THE PONY EXPRESS

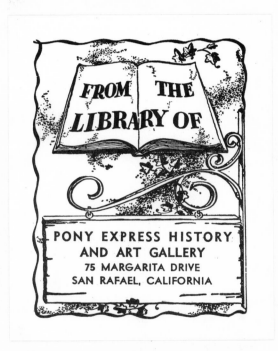

THE PONY EXPRESS

ILLUSTRATED WITH A UNIQUE COLLECTION OF HISTORICAL PICTURES

ASSEMBLED BY THE AUTHOR, LEE JENSEN

ORIGINAL DRAWINGS BY NICHOLAS EGGENHOFER

GROSSET & DUNLAP · PUBLISHERS · NEW YORK

EB

© COPYRIGHT 1955 BY A. L. JENSEN

PRINTED IN THE UNITED STATES OF AMERICA

rev, 7-17-86

CONTENTS

THE PONY EXPRESS

CHAPTER 1

THE PONY GOES THROUGH

IT WAS after seven in the morning, but the heavy gray clouds that hung over the Sierra Nevada Mountains obscured the April sun. Warren Upson glanced at his waiting horse, then studied the clouds with an anxious eye. He knew what they meant—*snow!* His ride would be the real test of the new Pony Express service.

Upson was waiting at the Sportsman's Hall express station on the western side of the Sierras. He would take over the mail from Bill Hamilton who had left Sacramento with the first Pony Express consignment, dated

[3]

The Pony Express

April 3, 1860, from San Francisco, California, to St. Joseph, Missouri. At St. Joe, the railroad from the East would take over.

The toughest part of the route started at Sportsman's Hall and continued on over the Sierras. Its weather was completely unpredictable. A sudden snowstorm beating down on a mountain pass could change familiar country into a strange and bewildering land in a matter of minutes. Even an experienced mountaineer could be hopelessly lost when all well-known landmarks were blotted out and he was forced to search for a new trail.

Warren Upson had been hand-picked for the Sierra run by Bolivar Roberts, who knew the territory and knew men. Roberts knew Upson to be an expert horseman and an experienced woodsman, who had roamed the mountain trails and passes from end to end in all seasons of the year.

Today, Upson's experience told him, he would need every minute of daylight to get across the mountains, and he listened intently for the hoofbeats of Hamilton's horse, hoping Bill had lost no time.

But Hamilton, like Upson and the other eighty riders stationed across the two-thousand-mile route, was a superb horseman, and he was keyed up to make this first trip his fastest.

The riverboat carrying the eastbound mail from San Francisco had docked in a rainy Sacramento shortly after two o'clock in the morning. At two-forty-five, after throwing the special mail pouch, called a "mochila," on his mount, Hamilton streaked east through the wet unlighted streets and out across the flat Sacramento valley. Because of the late hour, and perhaps the weather, only a few men at the station saw his departure. But the lack of fanfare would have no effect on his performance.

Hamilton had been allotted only four and one-half hours to travel forty-five miles to Placerville. The three relay stops between Sacramento and Placerville would consume a couple of minutes at least, and the muddy roads and trails would not allow any time to spare. He decided the level stretches of the Sacramento valley leading up to the American Fork would give him his only opportunity to gain a little extra time. He urged his horse on accordingly.

At Five Mile House the station men were waiting for him, so a few seconds were saved as he jumped out of one saddle and into another.

[4]

After two more stops, with fresh horses ready at Fifteen Mile House and Mormon Tavern, he began the gentle upgrade to Placerville. Hamilton thundered into the gold camp a full half hour earlier than he was expected. It was only six-forty-five. Ahead of him lay the final twelve miles. One more hour of fast riding and he was receiving the congratulations of the surprised people at Sportsman's Hall. He was ahead of time!

Upson didn't wait to join in the congratulations. Transferring the mochila to his own horse, he struck out up the trail. His run had been slated for daytime deliberately, for if the ride was tough by day, it was likely to be impossible by night. The schedule makers, however, could not foresee that this would be the day on which the mild winter would suddenly turn into a violent, freezing spring. That was exactly what was happening. Along the trail, doubts mounted hourly that the Pony would be able to get through the snow, which was piling higher and higher in the passes.

The Pony Goes Through

SIERRA SNOWSTORM

On past Hope Valley the trail became more and more hazardous. Upson had to be on guard constantly against slipping over an edge or into a canyon. He was all but blinded by the snow slapped into his face

[5]

The Pony Express

by the violent wind, and the familiar landmarks had disappeared under the heavy blanket of snow.

Upson knew he would have a constant battle with the weather until he reached Woodbridge and started down the eastern slopes of the Sierras. Skirting snowdrifts, trusting to luck and the instincts of his horse, he fought his way through the blizzard until he rode down out of a mountain pass onto level ground. To his great relief, he found himself once more on the wagon road.

With the snow banks now all behind him and his horse moving along at a great speed, he found it easier going the last fourteen miles into Carson City.

Upson had ridden about eighty-five miles over a trail most horsemen considered impassable and had worn out four horses on his way to Mormon Station alone. The townspeople of Carson City found it hard to believe he had really come across the mountains. He was a little behind schedule, but that was hardly noticed in the excitement of his arrival. It was plain that if the Pony could operate against these odds, nothing would be able to stop it.

The fact that Upson and all the riders that followed him got through with the mail came as a surprise to many of the people served by the Pony Express. Those who knew best what the express rider had to face voiced doubts that such a "crazy" plan could succeed. True, along the eastern part of the route near the Missouri river the riders would not run into much trouble. In the West it was a different story. With so many obstacles of harsh weather, uninhabited country, dangerous mountain trails, and warring Indians against it, the scheme seemed headed for certain disaster.

The heavy snows in the Sierras had always stopped all movement on the trails, so what chance could a lone rider on a difficult schedule have? And wouldn't the riders sent through Indian territory in Utah and Nevada most certainly be captured and scalped? Odds were offered in San Francisco that the entire plan would collapse before it got a good start.

But despite such gloomy predictions there was tremendous excitement following the announcement of the new service. For a long time Californians and other Westerners had felt their isolation deeply, and they had kept up a constant clamor for better mail service between East and West. The Pony Express, with its promise of news and mail from the East in ten days, offered even better service than they had hoped for. Nearly two weeks would be cut from the existing schedule for mail. It was inspiring even to think of this new kind of long-distance mail delivery, to be carried out by fleet horses and tireless riders.

For over a year and a half the Pony Express shuttled back and forth, carrying the fast mail both ways between the Missouri and the Pacific. A ceaseless, moving chain of horses and riders sped eastward and westward across two thousand miles that separated Saint Joseph and Sacramento. Stations dotted along the trail saw a regular series of arrivals and departures, day and night.

CHANGING HORSES

When a rider had completed his first stint of ten to twenty miles, he found a fresh horse waiting for him at a relay station. Four or five times, he would change from a tired mount to a new one, saddled and waiting to go. When a rider changed horses, so did the mochila, the lightweight, leather saddle blanket which had padlocked pockets for carrying the mail. It could be switched from one saddle to another in a few seconds.

The Pony Express

At the end of four or five short runs, the rider came to his 'home' station, where he handed the mochila over to another expressman, who then continued for another stretch. In this manner the mail passed from horse to horse and rider to rider, until it reached its destination.

Often two riders would pass each other on the trail. There would be just enough time for a wave and a shout of greeting when they met, for each rider was endeavoring to keep to a schedule of nine miles per hour. When the Pony Express was started, each rider was expected to

PASSING ON THE TRAIL

ride a stretch of forty or fifty miles, with two minutes allowed at each station for changing horses. The distance was extended to eighty or a hundred miles when the Pony began semi-weekly trips. And in case his relief rider became ill, a rider might have to carry on for two or three times his regular run.

The Pony Expressman carried a Colt revolver for protection from

[8]

Indians and outlaws, and even this weight was resented, for the lighter the burden the faster his horse could travel.

The station keepers, living in the lonely quarters dotted along the trail, in some respects had a worse time of it than the riders. There was very little excitement in the day-to-day routine of taking care of the horses and awaiting the next arrival of the Pony rider. In areas where the Indians were hostile, station keepers were in constant danger.

All day and all night, summer and winter, the mail was on its way. The Pony Express riders grew accustomed to being chased by Indians. They learned to take winter storm and desert heat in their stride and were not unduly alarmed by sudden blizzards and flooded rivers. They nearly always went through on schedule in spite of bad weather and Indian ambush.

Citizens of both the East and West soon grew to depend on the Pony Express for news of the world as well as for letters, both personal and business. The West, which had been starved for news for so long, began to feel it was really part of America, with the Pony racing back and forth across the wilderness.

When war between the North and South threatened, the Pony Express played a vital part in keeping the rich state of California in the Union. It was the Pony that carried the news of Abraham Lincoln's election in November of 1860 and the following spring speeded his great inaugural

The Pony Goes Through

SPEEDING THE NEWS

The Pony Express

message to the eagerly waiting Californians. In the black days at the beginning of the Civil War, news of the firing on Fort Sumter and the defeat at Bull Run were hurried to western presses. In Salt Lake City, the Deseret News put out a regular edition devoted solely to news brought by Pony Express.

The Pony Express lasted for only eighteen months—a brilliant and daring undertaking. The dauntless men who risked their lives for the Pony, were looked upon as heroes by their contemporaries and will always be seen in that light. Their brief careers made the Pony Express a symbol of speed and bold adventure that has never been equaled.

The Pony Goes Through

CHAPTER 2

THE LONG TREK FOR GOLD

AT FIRST no one believed the fantastic stories coming out of California. They were far too much like fairy tales. But the stories continued and by September, 1848, newspapers were printing them and a few people in the East had begun to pay attention. One man had become rich in a single day, just by picking up gold nuggets from the ground! Another had picked up a stone, and finding it exceptionally heavy for its size had examined it closely. It was almost pure gold! A woman had gone out with a dish pan and a kitchen knife and had dug three thou-

The Pony Express

sand dollars worth of gold out of a cliff in one afternoon! Anyone too lazy to go prospecting could hire Indians to do the work for him.

Everyone was interested in the new gold discoveries in California after President Polk spoke of them in a message to Congress in December. As physical proof of the abundance of gold, a box of gold flakes and lumps was put on display at the War Office. Crowds came daily to gape and marvel at the sight.

If the population of the eastern section of America was slow to believe the news from California, it had taken an even greater length of time for it to reach the East. For it had been nearly a year since James Marshal, a Mormon foreman overseeing some work near Sutter's Fort, had first spotted a flake of gold in the millrace and had debated whether to bother to pick it up.

Life at Sutter's Fort had been very peaceful before that eventful morning in January, 1848. Nine years earlier, John Sutter, a German-Swiss soldier of fortune, had managed to get a large grant of land from the Mexican Governor of California. He had convinced Governor Alvarado that he was the only man who could drive out the outlaws who infested the valleys around the Sacramento river. He would also hold in check the savage tendencies of the Indians who wandered the hills and streams. Alvarado gave him a vast grant of land at the junction of the Sacramento and American rivers. Along with the land went a small garrison of soldiers.

SUTTER'S FORT
It was a self-sufficient little kingdom. The fort's inhabitants produced everything they needed in its shops and on the land surrounding the Fort. There was always a garrison of soldiers on hand in case of trouble with the Indians or outlaws.

Sutter set about building a fort and establishing a self-sustaining community. A high wall of redwood logs surrounded a large dwelling, barracks for the soldiers and storage houses for the grains and provisions raised on his lands. The walled village stood among fields and vineyards. Men lived on horseback, looking after the sheep and cattle which ranged over thousands of acres. Cheeses, wool and stacks of hides, stiff as boards, were sent down the Sacramento River to the village of Yerba Buena, later to become San Francisco. From the ocean port they were shipped around Cape Horn to the East.

Sutter, who was usually addressed as Captain Sutter, lived like a feudal lord. The occasional trappers, emigrants or adventurers who straggled over the Sierras and down into the Sacramento valley enjoyed Sutter's hospitality and thought of him as a benign ruler of a little kingdom. They did not begrudge such a kind and generous man his great wealth. In 1848, when California passed to American ownership, Sutter's Fort was already the home of about one-fourth of the Americans living in California.

The Long Trek for Gold

BEAR HUNT
When the early Californians wanted to capture a bear for exhibition purposes, they went after him with lassos.

[15]

The Pony Express

The knowledge that California would be one of the states, sent no great wave of emigrants to its peaceful valleys, and for a while life at Sutter's Fort continued its easy-going way. But on the winter morning that James Marshal carried a little gold to the Fort to show to Sutter, that quietude changed to hysteria which gripped the entire nation and sent hordes of men trampling across Sutter's lands. Captain Sutter himself was the first to fall under the spell of the overwhelming news.

Mr. Marshal's appearance was in itself a surprise to Captain Sutter, who had only two days before sent him up the American river to do some work on a sawmill. Marshal's extreme excitement immediately prepared Sutter for some tale of calamity. Later, Sutter told of it this way:

"I was sitting one afternoon," said the Captain, "just after my siesta, engaged, by the bye, in writing a letter to a relation of mine in Lucerne, when I was interrupted by Mr. Marshal, a gentleman with whom I had frequent business transactions—bursting hurriedly into the room. From the unusual agitation in his manner I imagined that something serious had occurred, and, as we involuntarily do in this part of the world, I glanced to see if my rifle was in its proper place."

When Marshal announced without any preliminaries that they would both soon be wealthy beyond all reckoning, Sutter was sure he had taken leave of his wits. But when Marshal threw a handful of gold flakes on the table, Sutter was no longer skeptical and demanded the whole story.

He had followed Sutter's instructions for enlarging the millrace to the letter, Marshal related. When he had thrown the mill-wheel out of gear, the water had rushed from the dam through the narrow channel, tearing the dirt from its banks, leaving clean sides exposed. Early the next morning, while walking along the bank, he noticed something glit-

VAQUERO
Many of the vaqueros or herdsmen employed by Captain Sutter were Spanish or Mexican.

tering in the sand and gravel, but dismissed it as being some semi-precious stone, common in the area. When he noticed other shiny fragments, he idly picked one up to examine it. "Do you know," said Mr. Marshal, "I positively debated within myself two or three times, whether I should take the trouble to bend my back to pick up one of the pieces . . ." Marshal was certain that what he had found was a flake of pure gold. Gathering twenty or thirty pieces in secret, in order not to arouse the curiosity of the workmen, he decided to go straight to Captain Sutter with his find. He jumped on his horse and galloped to Sutter's Fort as fast as the animal would take him.

The Long Trek for Gold

SOCIAL LIFE
The Spanish who were living in California when gold was discovered loved music and dancing, and never missed an opportunity to have a party. They usually danced the fandango, a Spanish dance in waltz time.

Marshal and Sutter agreed to keep the discovery a secret and the following day they set off to explore the area surrounding the sawmill. For two days they wandered up the gulches and gullies, more and more elated over their findings. There was gold in abundance, not only in the streams but in every dried up creek bed and ravine. Overjoyed, they turned back toward the mill. Their dream of keeping this vast

[17]

The Pony Express

wealth for themselves had its first setback even as they came within sight of the mill.

Sutter wrote of it, ". . . as soon as we came back to the mill, we noticed by the excitement of the working people that we had been dogged about, and to complete our disappointment, one of the Indians who had worked at the gold mine in the neighborhood of La Paz, cried out in showing to us some specimens picked up by himself, 'Oro! Oro! Oro!' "

The secret was out. There was no longer any use to try to hide or diminish the limitless wealth hidden away in the hills. Men who could get there in a hurry from short distances flocked into the territory, abandoning all former activities. Trading ships carried the news to Hawaii, Mexico and South America. Sailors on their way to China and Australia talked of little else. Whalers, sailing the long fifteen thousand miles around Cape Horn, carried word of the discoveries to the East.

After President Polk's quiet recognition of the extent of the gold fields, Easterners were willing to believe any gold story, however extravagant. Doubts gave way to absurd credulity. It was generally believed that wealth lay there in untold amounts, ready to be plucked from the ground or panned from a clear mountain stream.

All over the nation, entire towns and villages were seized by the obsessive desire to get to California. In homes, stores, churches and town halls, all the talk was of gold. Just a little of it would lift a family out of the rut of drab day-to-day existence. This was the chance of a lifetime to get a little of the world's goods without grinding one's life away in the effort. Men by the thousands decided to have a try as quickly as possible. The only question remaining was how to get there in a hurry, before too many others.

Since it was winter, to go overland by wagon was out of the question. But almost overnight there appeared a variety of ships offering passage. Along the Atlantic coast and the Gulf of Mexico, every kind of seagoing craft, from shiny new steamers to rotted hulks ready for scuttling, was immediately put into use. Ship owners brought their schooners and brigs home from foreign trade and readied them for the more lucrative trip to California. Sometimes a few extra planks were built into a small coast-wise boat, enabling the owner to advertise it as "safe and comfortable."

Unless he could afford to travel in one of the new thousand-ton steamers just putting to sea for the first time, a man had to take what he could get when he applied for passage to California. He might find he had paid dearly for a miserable bunk in a completely unseaworthy ship. Men who pooled their capital and formed companies for the trip fared much better. They at least could buy their own boats, have decent repairs made and set out in an orderly fashion, well prepared for the unknown adventures ahead.

These companies, with fifty or a hundred or even more members, made up more than half of the first rush to the gold fields. For weeks, while they waited for the ships to be equipped, they held meetings, in which they formed by-laws for the groups and discussed every facet of sea travel and gold mining.

It was expensive to travel in any kind of comfort, expensive even to go at all. From seven-hundred to a thousand dollars had to be got for every man, the quicker the better. There were no limits to the ways the money could be found. Business establishments and homes were sold for half what they were worth in order to finance the journey. Tight-fisted townsmen, who had never spent a cent on anything except the

The Long Trek for Gold

ROUND THE HORN TO CALIFORNIA
For years after the discovery of gold, ships traveling around Cape Horn would be swamped with requests for passage.

[19]

The Pony Express

necessary food and shelter, drew their life's savings out of the bank and splurged on mining equipment and clothing to wear in the camps.

Pawnbrokers were busy day and night striking good bargains with needy customers. Well-to-do gentlemen, who for reasons of age, health or security, preferred to stay safely at home, staked a dozen or more young men, better qualified for the ordeal. Many a young man signed away a share of the gold he might never see in return for financial backing.

By January of 1849, factories, farms and shops in the East were losing their employees to the gold fever so rapidly that they were facing a serious labor shortage. At the same time, the demands for clothing, foods and all kinds of hard goods from guns to shovels became enormous. The Forty-niner, making ready to sail for strange ports, did a thorough job of outfitting himself.

On the advice of strangers, usually shopkeepers with no more knowledge of California than himself, he invested heavily in a wide assortment of boots, coats and trousers (extra heavy or flimsily light), weapons, provisions for the journey, and miner's goods. Some took along untested and useless devices for washing gold, clumsy machines which would be dumped unused on the California beaches and hills.

Soon the harbors along the Atlantic coast and the Gulf of Mexico were crowded with hundreds of ships making ready for the departure for California. Any kind of craft that could stay afloat could fill its passenger list in a matter of hours. Greedy ship owners jammed their vessels with mountains of cargo and packed them to bursting with men who had no choice but to crowd into any kind of dark corner they were offered. They put to sea, some for the long route around Cape Horn, others for a port on the Isthmus of Panama.

The firm belief that he was on his way to make his fortune, carried the early Argonaut through a lot of misery in the weeks and months ahead. A great deal of dry hardtack and rancid meat could be washed down with stale water and forgotten; a lot of seasickness and boredom could be endured so long as he was confident that it was only a matter of time before he would be rich and powerful. If any traveler ever needed fantastic dreams to buoy him up, the early Forty-niner was that man. Crowded into ships originally built for half the number they were carrying, the eager landlubbers fought to get their sea legs, were laid low by seasickness, were sometimes forced to the point of mutiny after facing daily a diet of salt meat, dried fish, beans and hardtack. The terrible lack of privacy was hard enough to bear. In the cramped quarters, there was no escape from the masses of restless, noisy emigrants.

It was fifteen thousand miles to California by way of Cape Horn, and the blunt-nosed sailing ships took from five to seven months to complete the journey. Through every extreme of tropical heat and antarctic winter, the ships slowly plowed their way toward Cape Horn. In the constant battle with violent storms the ships sometimes consumed a month in rounding the Cape. Mountainous seas rolled and plunged under the light vessels, and the wrecks of earlier ships were often seen, keeping the passengers in constant awareness of their peril. Almost as bad as the terror while sailing around the Cape, was the tedium. Week after week, the travelers looked at the same faces, ate the same monotonous diet which grew steadily worse as the voyage lengthened and supplies dwindled.

The Long Trek for Gold

STEAMER ARRIVAL

Gold seekers who went to California by way of the Isthmus of Panama boarded a side-wheeler for the trip up the coast to San Francisco. The arrival of a steamer was the occasion for much excitement.

[21]

The Pony Express

However dangerous and boring the Cape Horn passage might be, it was for a short while the route to California taken by the majority of the voyagers. The alternate route by way of the Isthmus of Panama cut several thousand miles from the distance to California but somewhere near the middle of that journey there was a fifty-mile jungle to be crossed. Only those most eager to be in the vanguard cared to risk its dangers.

Day after day the traveler sat in native boats on the Chagres river or rode a mule through steaming swampland, as he crossed from the Atlantic to the Pacific side of the narrow Isthmus. If he did not contract yellow fever or malaria he was lucky. But even if he arrived at Panama City, on the Pacific shore, in a sound condition, he might have to wait weeks or months for passage up the coast to San Francisco. Many discouraged emigrants turned back to the states, and most of them wondered why they had not waited until spring, when the overland route would be open to wagon traffic.

In the early spring of 1849, even before the winter snows had entirely disappeared, the frontier settlements along the Missouri river began to take on a new character. Covered wagons filled the streets and overflowed into the marshy river-bottom lands. Gold seekers bound for California turned the towns into rushing cities as they went about the important business of outfitting for the weeks ahead. Men haggled in the brand new shops over the exorbitant prices being charged for picks and shovels, bacon and beans. Owners of hardware stores and saddle and harness shops sold out their stocks again and again and had to wait impatiently for new shipments. Ambitious young men who could not afford to buy a wagon to carry them west, were busy seeking jobs with large wagon trains.

Over the bustle sounded the clang of the blacksmith's anvil, the cracking of whips and bellowing of oxen, the hundred banging, pounding noises of building and repairing. Storekeepers, servants, preachers, laborers, lawyers, mechanics, were awaiting the right moment for starting the long journey to California.

The day for starting was chosen with the utmost pains. Only the wagon trains which took grain along could set forth without anxiety as soon as spring arrived. The others must be sure the grass would be high enough to feed the animals by the time they reached the plains.

By the first day of May wagons were straggling out of the towns and others just like them were taking their places. Every trail known to lead westward was soon lined with white-topped emigrant wagons, crowding each other in their haste to reach the gold fields before autumn. Some followed the Santa Fe Trail south and then turned west to California. Others took a trail which swung far south through Texas and the southwestern deserts. But mostly they went by the route which led up the Platte River to the mountains, the Oregon-California road. Caravan after caravan left the woods behind and climbed slowly up to the dry plains. In custom-built heavy wagons, well furnished as a dwelling, in rickety vehicles barely able to roll, in any kind of conveyance that would get them to California, the emigrants streamed across the prairies, now turning green in the spring sunlight.

A few days west of the Missouri River, a wagon train would stop for a while to get its bearings. It was at this time that the wagon master or captain was elected, to take on the responsibility of seeing the train through the entire trip. These elections were often the cause of violent quarrels, for there were many men who thought they should have the job, many who thought they alone could carry the wagon party through the annoyances and emergencies sure to arise.

If it did not run into trouble, a train could cover ten to fifteen miles each day. The emigrant's day began when he was awakened before dawn. Usually the oxen were yoked at once and without waiting to eat breakfast the train was on its way. Late in the morning the company stopped, turned out the animals to graze, and built fires for cooking a meal of flapjacks, bacon and coffee. Families who had brought chickens along would have eggs occasionally.

After a long afternoon and evening of travel, the wagons were skillfully maneuvered into position to form a corral, either circular or square, which would serve as a sort of fortress for the company. Within its protective walls, formed by the heavy wagons chained closely together, all the social life of the group was carried on. Women prepared meals while the children played games just as though they were at home. Church services were held in the enclosure, and if there was a fiddler in the company, young people sometimes enjoyed a dance.

In the early crossing of the plains there were few Indian scares but there were other terrors to be lived through. Prairie storms were as

The Long Trek for Gold

[23]

WAGON TRAINS PLIED THE TRAILS STEADIL

THROUGH THE SUMMER AND FALL OF 1849

ROUGH GOING
By the time the wagons reached the Sierras the tired oxen needed all the help they could get. Men walked beside the wagons and pushed their wagons when they came to a steep spot.

much to be feared as any wild Indians. Rain fell in solid sheets and the high winds ripped the canvas covers from the wagon frames, leaving the travelers wet and shivering. Cloudbursts turned tiny streams into rivers that were almost impossible to ford.

Fear of stampede was always with the emigrants. For the slightest reason or sometimes no apparent reason at all, oxen, horses and mules would be overtaken by a frenzy of excitement and break for some distant goal, letting the wagons they were drawing follow as best they might.

As the agitation of the few spread like wildfire through the wagon trains, every animal would be infected until nothing but fear existed. And fear communicated itself, too, to the trapped passengers of the lurching schooners, who were unable to stop the animals, unable even to jump from the wagons for fear of being trampled by the maddened creatures just behind.

Beyond Fort Laramie, the emigrants began to get rid of everything they could, in order to lighten the load for the tired draft animals. Farm machinery, favorite pieces of furniture, trunks of clothing, all intended for the new life in California were dumped beside the trail.

When the emigrants crossed the deserts of Utah and Nevada they encountered the worst conditions on the trail. Here there was no escape from the merciless heat and when water was finally found it often proved to be poisonous with alkali. It was in these deserts that men abandoned worn-out animals and wrecked wagons, and made a last desperate effort to reach the Sierras.

For once over that barrier and safely down its western slopes, they could easily scatter through the gold fields, each man to search out his own particular fortune.

Few, if any, of these Forty-niners thought of themselves as settlers. They came to California to make their fortunes in gold and then they planned to return home to lord it over their old neighbors in luxury. Thus their thoughts, aside from gold, remained centered around the East and they were eager for any means of communication with home. But communication between the West and East was so slow and uncertain as to be practically worthless.

The Long Trek for Gold

CHAPTER 3

JACKASS AND STAGECOACH

IN THE DAYS following the discovery of gold in California, the only reasonably sure way of sending mail from East to West was by sea. A letter mailed in the East took a long and precarious journey before it finally reached its addressee in California or Oregon. It first went by boat to Panama, and was carried across the jungle and swamplands of the Isthmus of Panama to the Pacific Ocean. The Pacific Mail Steamship line then took over the mailbags for the slow trip up the coast to San Francisco.

[29]

The Pony Express

The only thing certain about the mail delivery was that the letters and newspapers would be at least a month to six weeks old. No one could ever tell exactly when the Pacific Mail steamships would arrive. This was the reason San Franciscans looked toward Telegraph Hill so anxiously. For on the Hill stood the semaphore which gave the signal that a side-wheeler was finally steaming into harbor. When the semaphore arms went up, there was a general rush to the Post Office and the queuing-up began. One might stand in line for hours before he collected his mail, unless he could buy a spot at the head of the line. Selling his place in the line was one way a needy citizen could always earn a little money.

The gold rush, that world-shaking event which changed San Francisco from a sleepy village into a roaring town, had created scores of lesser towns and villages. By the middle of 1849 prospectors had pushed

SAN FRANCISCO POST OFFICE
San Franciscans were weary of mob scenes at the Post Office, but there was no way to avoid them since every man wanted his mail immediately.

[30]

far up the streams into the gold country. The branches of the Sacramento and San Joaquin rivers and the creeks and streams that fed them were alive with the efforts of industrious miners. Gold camps of tents and shacks sprang up by the score. On the pine-dotted hills and in the rocky canyons, settlements made up almost entirely of men appeared overnight. Land that had been ignored by the Mexicans and left to a few small bands of Indians, had become priceless beyond reckoning.

The rough, new camps had little to offer except back-breaking labor.

Jackass and Stagecoach

PACK MULES
Mule trains carried all heavy mining equipment and supplies up into the hills.

There were no roads whatsoever into the gold region. In the early days any contact with the outside world was rare and more or less accidental. Pack-mule trains, climbing the slopes from the Sacramento valley, sometimes brought extremely out-of-date newspapers and letters along with the mining tools and provisions.

The preposterous names of the little towns that sprang into being came out of the broad humor that turned hardship and deprivation into a joke. But they also suggest these were to be temporary stops, some

The Pony Express

place to get rich before returning to a more conventional life. Jackass Flat, Dead Man's Gulch, Lousy Level and Slapjack Bar; Ground Hog's Glory, Murderer's Bar, Whiskey Hill and Henpeck Flat; these were not names even the young, reckless population of California would have given to a spot it actually considered home.

Someplace else that had been left behind was still considered home by the uprooted people living in California in the years following the gold rush. They had come there to find gold, the sooner the better. In the meantime, next to making a rich strike very quickly, the most desirable thing in the world was news of families and friends left behind. A letter arriving at the mines was read and reread, not only by the owner but by his companions, until it was no longer decipherable.

More often than not, letters wound up in the dead letter office in San Francisco. Hundreds of pounds stacked up every time the mail

SACRAMENTO HILLS
Every gully and mountain pass in the gold regions was explored and searched for possible gold finds.

ship came into port, for nine times out of ten the addressee was not on hand to collect his mail. It was not that he did not want it desperately, for he would have walked the hundred or so miles from the camp to the Post Office, if he had had the time to spare. But of necessity, he was up some remote gulch or ravine, slaving away with gold pan or pick and shovel. The precious letter, already a month or more old, thus had another delay of weeks or months before it found its way up into the mines.

Towns were springing up and prospectors pouring into the territory so fast that the Post Office Department had lost control of the situation. Some way had to be found for getting the mail out of San Francisco to outlying camps. Since official postmen were nonexistent, it was inevitable that self-appointed ones should appear to fill the need. And so came into being the colorful "Jackass Express" with its scores of "companies," consisting of a man and a mule, or sometimes only a lone man, who strode up the mountain passes with seventy or eighty pounds of mail on his back.

The first of these California "expresses" of any consequence started operation in July of 1849. Alexander H. Todd, who had come to California by sea only a month before, abandoned his original plans for

Jackass and Stagecoach

DIGGINGS
Far from being a romantic pastime, gold mining, in the early days at least, was a matter of hard pick-and-shovel labor.

[3 3]

The Pony Express

gold mining and went into business for himself. He had noticed how eagerly miners looked forward to the rare mail delivery, and also their bitter disappointment when it failed to arrive. Todd rode a mule into Sonora, Mokelumne Hill, and other settlements in the southern gold area. He talked to the miners and found they were more than willing to pay him well for bringing their mail from the Post Office in San Francisco. Each one gave him a dollar when his name was registered,

SALOON

Most of the social life in the gold camps and towns centered around the saloon and gambling hall.

and promised an ounce of gold dust upon receiving his letters and parcels. As an ounce of dust was worth from fifteen to eighteen dollars, Todd could not fail to grow rich at a greater rate than most miners.

On his first trip out of the mines, some of the citizens of Stockton asked him if he would carry a few packages down to San Francisco for deposit with Ford & Company. Todd was amazed to discover that the makeshift bags and boxes turned over to him contained gold dust worth the huge

FLAPJACKS

In camps where there were no women, miners soon got used to doing their own cooking and housekeeping.

sum of $250,000. This consignment had been entrusted without hesitation to a man most of the shippers had never seen before.

The only thing Todd could find to pack it in was an old butter keg. In this fashion the precious dust traveled down the river to San Francisco. For this service Todd received five per cent of the amount carried, or $12,500.

In San Francisco, Todd was sworn in as a Postal clerk, collected all the mail addressed to his clients, bought all the New York newspapers he could carry. Back in the mines, he sold the papers for eight dollars a copy.

The Postmaster, seeing a chance to cut in on a little of this wealth for himself, began to assess Todd a quarter on each letter taken from

Jackass and Stagecoach

SATURDAY NIGHT DANCE
After a week of labor the miners enjoyed a dance on Saturday night. Some of the miners played the part of the 'lady'. The 'ladies' could be recognized by the patches on their trousers. But the bearded men swung their partners with as much enthusiasm as if they were attending a regular party.

[3 5]

The Pony Express

the Post Office. To keep his express running smoothly, he could afford to give the Postmaster this small rake-off. He also paid the legitimate postage on letters from the States, at that time amounting to forty cents on each letter.

Such fantastic profits made the express business seem extremely attractive, and dozens of express companies sprang into existence. In a short while competition had forced prices down to a saner level, and the expressman had become a fixture of camp life.

No one ever enjoyed a more free and independent life. The expressman was president, secretary and treasurer of his company rolled into one, and answered to no one. Every gold camp had its regular visits, and the arrival of the expressman, bringing news of home and friends was the high point in the miner's life.

Alonzo Delano, who was an expressman himself, wrote in *Penknife Sketches:*

"The Express has arrived! Every pick and shovel is dropped, every pan is laid aside, every rocker is stopped with its half-washed dirt, every claim is deserted, and they crowd around the store with eager enquiries, 'Have you got a letter for me?' With what joy it is seized, and they care little whether they pay two or five dollars for it, they've got a letter. Or perhaps, as is often the case, the answer is 'There's nothing for you,' and with a 'Damn the luck' and a heavy heart, they go sullenly back to work, unfitted by disappointment for social intercourse the rest of the day."

A miner did not stick to a claim unless it paid off quickly. He would constantly move about in order to try his luck in fresh diggings. Sometimes a letter would follow him from camp to camp, passing through the hands of so many expressmen that it was all but pulverized by the time he got

MOUNTAIN EXPRESSMAN
The expressman, bringing the mail, was the most welcome visitor in the mines.

[36]

it. Over hill, ridge and gulch, the California expressmen rode or walked, getting to know every name in the camps along their routes.

In less than a year after Todd's start, the expresses were considered so reliable that miners were using the company names as mailing addresses. The companies even furnished hand-stamped stationery to those who wanted it. Printed on the envelopes were the name, route

Jackass and Stagecoach

BAD NEWS
All work was abandoned when the mail arrived in the camps. For a little while the miners were transported to another world as they read their letters from home and exchanged gossip. Bad news was harder to take, so far from home and friends.

and a suitable emblem, the better to advertise the line. Zack's Snowshoe Express, for instance, run by Granville Zachariah of Downieville, used the appropriate picture of a man on snowshoes, traveling through the mountains.

With dozens of expresses springing up like mushrooms after rain, the problem of mail delivery to the Sierra foothills had been taken care

The Pony Express

of very efficiently and promptly. But if Californians expected anything similar to take place in the handling of the long distance routes, they were to be greatly disappointed. However bitter they might be toward the Pacific Mail Steamship Line, that long route by water was to remain for many years the safest, surest way of sending a letter between East and West.

In the first years of California's rise, our Post Office Department did not deliver the mail to the West. Instead, contracts were made with private companies or individuals to carry the mail to a few post offices then in existence. These contracts were eagerly competed for—although

In 1855 the forty-seven-mile railroad across the Isthmus of Panama was completed, and the mails from East and West were speeded up a little.

for years they were completely inadequate. The failures, both tragic and absurd, that dotted the 1850's were due to lack of backing, rather than any shortage of courage or imagination on the part of the carriers. For the early contractors were there ready to brave any danger in their efforts to get the mails through.

In 1850 Samuel H. Woodson left Missouri with a wagon-load of mail and packages destined for Salt Lake City. This was the first time that the United States government had ever granted a contract for carrying the mails overland across the continent. It called for monthly service between Independence, Missouri, and Salt Lake City. Woodson found that even this schedule could not be met. There were no relay stations along the way so the same mule teams worked through the entire trip. Resting at night and traveling by day, Woodson made very slow progress over the miserable roads. The Mormons had a very poor opinion of the slow and irregular service given them from the East. But it was all they were to have for several years.

The next year a similar service was begun between California and the Mormon capital. George Chorpenning and Absolom Woodward contracted to cover the seven-hundred miles between Sacramento and Salt Lake City twice in thirty days. Their story is a catalogue of every obstacle of weather and Indian trouble known on the trails. Although it was well into spring when they left Sacramento, they traveled through deep snow for sixteen days and slept on the snow at night. Unlike wagon trains which carried supplies and could safely camp out until the going was easier, pack mules had to keep moving no matter what the conditions of the trail.

The following November disaster nearly ended Chorpenning's line before it had got a good start. Woodward, with a party of five men, made his way to within one-hundred and fifty miles of Salt Lake City, where they were seen by emigrants near Willow Springs. They then dropped from sight and nothing more was heard of them all winter. In May the snows had disappeared and search parties were sent out to look for them. Their arrow-pierced bodies, found by the little squad of searchers, made it all too clear what had happened to them.

On another trip, a group of Chorpenning's men, slowed by blizzard and freezing weather, spent fifty-three days on the road. When their animals froze to death, and their provisions gave out, they handled the

Jackass and Stagecoach

[39]

The Pony Express

crisis in true pioneer fashion. They cut up the carcasses for meat, packed it on their backs with the mail, and walked the remaining two hundred miles into Salt Lake City.

Chorpenning's service was never successful. At one point the danger of Indian attack was so great that he could not persuade his men to go out. In order to save his contract he made the entire trip alone, through country where it was definitely known that Indians were on the lookout for white men's scalps. Forced by recurring blizzards to use a more southern and longer route for part of the year, his line became even more unsatisfactory.

Through the years Congress was constantly besieged by demands for better communications. The constant pressure gave rise to some extremely wild ideas. One of the most fantastic schemes centered around the Saharan camel and its use as a beast of burden in the great American desert. Camels seemed the perfect answer to the problem of transporting mail and freight across the hot southwestern deserts.

BALKY CAMEL
Camels taken on the U. S. store-ship Supply *hated the sight of water and had to be coaxed onto the boat.*

They were fleet and strong and used to traveling across hot sands. They could march long distances without water, could even eat the desert cactus. Surely nothing could be more suited for the wide stretches of Utah and Nevada.

The subject was brought up in Congress for three successive years before a sum of money was set aside for the project. Plans were made to import camels and also their native caretakers.

A small group of military men was sent to London by Jefferson Davis, the Secretary of War. There they studied the habits and care of camels at the London zoo, before sailing in the U.S. Store-ship *Supply*. Three months later in the spring of 1856, the *Supply* was back with 33 camels in the hold.

A camel train was sent with a detachment of soldiers from Texas to California. This trip was to prove once and for all that camels would be an ideal means of carrying mail and supplies in the desert. By this time most of the camel tenders had disappeared and the complaining soldiers were forced to feed and pack both mules and camels. Soon the camels were suffering from sore backs brought on by carrying heavy and badly balanced loads. They had sore feet from walking long distances over the hard-packed trails, so different from the soft flowing sands of the Sahara. Outfitted with leather boots, they were even more

Jackass and Stagecoach

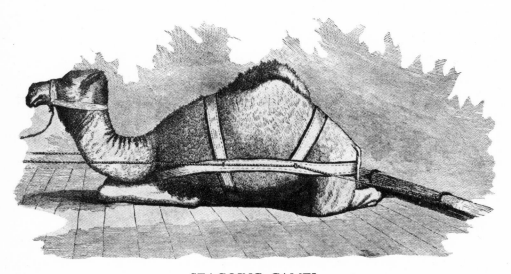

SEAGOING CAMEL
When the seas were rough the camels were tied down to the ship's deck in a kneeling position, so they would not break their legs.

helpless. Furthermore horses and mules were terrified by the strange beasts and the constant runaways added to the confusion.

Although by the end of the expedition the camels were greatly admired for their patience and endurance, they were sent to a ranch in Bakersfield, until some other use could be found for them. The shrinking of the desert was left to more practical thinkers.

The Pony Express

In 1857 a letter could be sent overland from East to West, but it traveled in uncertain, piecemeal fashion, passing from one contractor to another. W. M. F. McGraw, Hiram Kimball, S. B. Miles, and Hockaday and Liggett all contracted to carry the mail west of the Missouri at one time or another.

At one time Californians sent Congress a petition pleading for some better means of communication—seventy-five thousand signatures went along with it to Washington.

The West's demands for a single, efficient mail service had grown more persistent each year. In 1857 the Overland Mail Bill, providing for just such a service, was finally passed in Congress, with the choice of route still undecided. But official Washington had been stirred into action only partially by the desire to accommodate the frontier. In the background were other considerations that made the establishing of a direct mail route urgent. The quarrel between North and South over the question of slavery was growing hotter daily. Leaders of both factions tried to strengthen their positions as they saw war coming closer and closer. The great wealth of gold-producing California was seen in a new light. In case of conflict, whoever controlled California would have an enormous advantage.

The choice of a route west now became all important. If it ran through the South, the slave-holding Southerners would be in control of all contact with the West. If the route took the shorter and logical central road up the Platte and over South Pass, the North would increase its strength and keep California in the Union.

The general public also had a strong interest in where the route would lie. Most people believed that the future railroad to the Pacific would follow the path of the first Overland Mail coaches. And there was not a village west of the Missouri that did not want to be on that railroad.

The administration under President Buchanan was thoroughly Southern in its sympathies, and the new Postmaster General, Aaron V. Brown, was from the Southern state of Tennessee. So when Postmaster Brown selected a route which dipped far to the South, no one was very surprised. A contract was granted to John Butterfield, an experienced freighter and a friend of President Buchanan, to operate a semi-weekly mail delivery between the Missouri and the Pacific.

The Butterfield route was long and round-about. Two branches started in Memphis and St. Louis and met at Fort Smith, Ark. A single road then formed a great arc through Oklahoma, Texas and Arizona to California.

In the North and West, the choice of an almost untraveled road, nearly a thousand miles out of the way, was furiously denounced. Before long the line was spoken of derisively as the "Ox-Bow Route." The acidly humorous name derived appropriately from the hair-pin like curve of the bows that encircled the necks of yoked oxen. This new line bypassed Salt Lake City by hundreds of miles and left Sacramento completely out of the picture. The Sacramento Union referred to it as "a Panama route by land." Postmaster Brown defended his peculiar choice by pointing out that the Central Route had been proven impassable in winter and that the country was infested with Indians. He failed to add that no contractor taking that route had ever had enough government backing to equip himself properly. No real attempt had ever been made to develop the road.

The Butterfield coaches, painted bright red or green, and drawn by four mules, carried both passengers and mail. From nine to fourteen people could be carried in the body of the coach, and up in front with the driver another passenger or two could be squeezed in. In the rear

Jackass and Stagecoach

FORDING STREAM
The Butterfield route was long and arduous. While much of it was desert, in flood season every tiny stream turned into a river that had to be cautiously forded.

[4 3]

The Pony Express

of the coach, in the triangular "boot," were stowed all luggage and mail bags. The overflow from the "boot" went inside, under the seats or under the uncomfortable passengers' feet. Mail bags were even carried at times between the axles and the body of the coach, with disastrous results to printed matter in wet weather.

The Ox-Bow Route ran through country where Comanches and Apaches were constantly on the war path. The isolated stations were besieged by their raiding parties, and scalping stock-tenders became a regular business. Snow was not a problem, but the summers were fiercely hot. Way passengers crowded into the coaches, adding to the misery of the travelers who had started out from the eastern termini in comparative comfort. One passenger said, at the end of the line, "I know what hell is like. I've had twenty-five days of it."

RUNAWAY
No matter how a stage driver lashed his horse, the stages could cover only a short distance each day.

A Dr. Tucker, who sat in a Butterfield stage all the way from the Missouri River to the Pacific Ocean, wrote of his journey and the perils of stage travel for the San Francisco *Argonaut*. Bowling along through Arkansas, he was luxuriating in the roominess of a coach occupied by only two men other than himself. The situation was far too good to last. He wrote:

> Shortly after crossing the Red River, we took aboard a party of four—two men and two women—all French . . . The younger man of about thirty-five years, was evidently a Parisian—a haughty, supercilious fellow, who saw nothing but the young and handsome French girl . . .

> Somewhere about here, we took on a typical border man—a tall, handsome young fellow, in boots and buckskins, bound for his ranch in Texas. With western familiarity, he was at once addressed as "Texas," as I was saluted as "California."

> A few miles further and a fat German boarded us. . . He was immediately christened "Dutchy" by the Texan.

This international group filled the coach to its limits. The cast had been assembled but its members had not yet begun to show their true characters. All went well until a torrential rain storm made it necessary to close the windows. In the sweltering heat the coach was suffocating. Each passenger began to feel uncomfortable.

Jackass and Stagecoach

BIVOUAC
Sometimes emigrants were seen camping out along the lonely Ox-Bow route.

The Pony Express

The Americans passed around their flasks, joked and told stories. The Frenchmen distantly rejected, in French, all approach at companionship, while Dutchy disagreeably growled at the want of room and air.

To while away the time, the Texan began paying attention to the younger and prettier of the two French women. By the time the stage reached Texarkansas, the flirtation had reached a critical point and the French suitor was in a rage. Dutchy had begun to smoke a huge, odorous pipe. Texas, now settled in his role of gallant, snatched the pipe from the fat man's lips and threw it out the window. Dutchy was eager to start a fight, but there was hardly enough room to move in such close quarters, so he choked off his anger with a drink from his flask, and went to sleep with his back against the door.

His snoring was equal to trombone practice and so annoying that Texas finally said: "We'll have to get shut of this porker."

Quietly reaching behind Dutchy, he turned the door-catch nearly around. The next jolt . . . the door gave way, and out went Dutchy, heels over head into the road.

Texas at once sprang out, helped him up, and in a tone of bantering solicitude, inquired if he was hurt. Dutchy fairly foamed with rage and charged us all with an attempt to kill him. So violent was he that we would not allow him to re-enter the stage, insisting on his riding outside . . .

Dutchy was left behind at the next station but only part of the tension in the coach disappeared with him. As the stage rolled across the Texas plains, the feud between Texas and the French girl's admirer became hotter and hotter. Texas' attentions to the girl were interrupted from time to time by bursts of denunciation from the Frenchman, who forgot himself and shouted abuses in English instead of French.

In the early evening the coach pulled up to the station where the passengers were to eat supper. There was to be a long wait for some of them, however, for it was at this moment that the insulted Frenchman demanded 'satisfaction' and a duel to the death was arranged between him and the reckless Texan. Dr. Tucker acted as a second in Texas' behalf, and the duel was fought with revolvers in a corral back of the station. He wrote this graphic account:

[46]

Sheltered by the heavy gate-posts from flying balls, we seconds watched the principals, who cautiously walked toward each other across the broad corral. While the Frenchman, with upraised pistol, and eyes gleaming malignant hatred, was edging sideways across the tract, Texas was carelessly and more rapidly approaching him with square front.

Suddenly the Frenchman dropped his revolver and quickly fired two shots. At the second discharge, Texas half-wheeled to the left and staggered. His exposed left arm was shattered near the wrist . . .

The blood was pouring from Texas' wounded arm as he again sprang several yards nearer his antagonist, who paused, and they quickly fired together. The Frenchman's shot knocked off Texas' hat; but as yet the Frenchman was unhurt

Jackass and Stagecoach

BUTTERFIELD COACH
The Butterfield line was well-managed and well-equipped so the coaches usually ran on time.

[47]

The Pony Express

Then Texas dropped upon one knee, and setting his revolver across his wounded arm, fired with deliberate aim. His antagonist was, at the moment, also in the act of firing, but Texas' bullet reached his heart before he could press the trigger. Throwing his arms wildly in the air, the Frenchman fell dead.

The firing had attracted all of the inmates of the station—not more than half a dozen. These—with the two French women—quickly surrounded the fallen man. The driver had eaten his supper, fresh horses were in the harness, and Texas and myself could only squeeze some food and jump into the coach, as the six wild mustangs started off on a fierce gallop. I also carried off the roller-towel and some shingles to splint the broken arm.

The Butterfield line could never be comfortable or fast, but it was reliable. The stages kept on schedule amazingly well, usually taking from twenty-one to twenty-three days for the trip. The huge yearly subsidy of $600,000 had enabled Butterfield to equip his line handsomely with the best coaches and mules.

The most severe criticism of the Butterfield line had never been directed at the way it was operated, but rather at the route itself. The fault-finding continued and became even more vociferous when a whole new area of the West stirred to life with the finding of gold in Colorado . . . the Pike's Peak gold discoveries. A new flood of emigrants now took to the trail. Some followed the Santa Fe Trail to Bent's Old Fort on the Arkansas River and then turned north to Cherry Creek, in the Pike's Peak area. Others took to the Oregon Trail or the shorter, but Indian-infested Smoky Hill Route straight across the plains. "Fifty-niners" painted "Pike's Peak or Bust" on their wagon tops and hurried toward the Colorado plateau. Some even walked the seven hundred miles from the Missouri River, pushing their belongings ahead of them in handcarts, or carrying packs on their backs.

Denver and Auraria went up on opposite banks of Cherry Creek and competed to attract the incoming hordes. Thousands flocked up Russell Gulch and Gregory Gulch to try their luck in the little streams that meandered through the foothills.

In this new El Dorado, it was the same story as in California a decade before. In the new, raw camps a demand for some kind of communication with the East arose almost at once. The area was far removed from any mail route, and two hundred miles from the nearest Post Office at Fort Laramie. For a few months after the first excitement, a trader, Jim Saunders, carried mail and newspapers back and forth between Denver and Fort Laramie. Each trip consumed about six weeks.

Jackass and Stagecoach

EARLY DENVER
For a little while after gold was found on Cherry Creek, Denver was only a shack town.

William Larimer, who helped to found the city of Denver, described this slow and primitive means of sending a letter in his *Reminiscences:*

> Jim Saunders, who had roamed all over the West with his Indian family, said he would go to the Post Office for us if we would give him fifty cents for each letter and twenty-five cents for each paper; so he got a list of all the names of persons in our district and on 23 November started with his squaw in a little wagon drawn by four Indian ponies for his two-hundred mile journey.

To a man just arrived from the East, six weeks seemed an eternity to go without letters and news. Citizens of the new boom towns hardly knew who was to blame, Jim Saunders or the contractors who brought the mail from the East to Fort Laramie.

The Pony Express

Among the many Western freighters and promoters who had been watching the activity around Pike's Peak, was William H. Russell, a partner in the freighting firm of Russell, Majors and Waddell. Russell was eager to run a daily mail coach from Leavenworth, Kansas, to Den-

GREGORY GULCH WAS THE DESTINATIO

ver. His idea started a chain of events which would end only when letters and news could be moved with lightning speed. For it was the daring Russell, always ready for a gamble, who was destined to be the author of one of the most romantic chapters in western history.

F THOUSANDS OF THE "FIFTY-NINERS"

CHAPTER 4

THE BOLD PLAN

William H. Russell was one of three partners in the firm of Russell, Majors and Waddell, the greatest freighting outfit on the plains. When Russell, a born promoter, first broached the subject of a daily stage line between Leavenworth, Kansas, and Denver, his partners were dead set against the idea. The proposed line, they argued, would be an expensive one to operate and equip, and all the money would have to come out of their own pockets, since no mail contract with the government

The Pony Express

had been obtained. And then, if the gold discoveries in Colorado should prove to be a fluke, their entire investment would be lost.

Russell, not to be discouraged, separately joined with a new partner, John Jones, a freighter of Missouri, and formed the Leavenworth and Pike's Peak Express Company. In early 1859, this newly fledged firm went in debt for fifty beautiful Concord coaches and eight hundred or more fine Kentucky mules and began daily stages to Denver. The service and treatment of the passengers were excellent, with hot meals served at comfortable stations along the way.

In Denver, there were grumblings about the high prices paid for passenger tickets and express. A letter went for only twenty-five cents, but a one-way ticket was $125, and packages cost a dollar a pound. In spite of these high prices, it soon became apparent that the Leavenworth and Pike's Peak Express was running deeply in debt. It was costing a thousand dollars a day to run the line, and still the looked-for mail contract was nowhere in sight. When their notes fell due, they could not pay them. The firm of Russell, Majors and Waddell came to the rescue, bought up the Jones and Russell notes and became owners of the stage line.

The lavish stages to Denver and now also to Salt Lake City continued to whirl along at a rate of one hundred and twenty miles every

DENVER STAGE
The stages to Denver rolled along both day and night and passengers got whatever sleep they could in the swaying, rocking coaches.

twenty-four hours. For the first time in history it was possible to enjoy a trip across the plains. In February, 1860, the coaches started running all the way to the Pacific, and the company took on the lengthy name of Central Overland California and Pike's Peak Express Company, usually referred to as the C.O.C. and P.P. Exp. Co.

Though there had never been anything like it before, the new line simply did not pay. No stage line could break even without the help of a government subsidy. Butterfield, still sending coaches along the Ox-Bow Route in the South, could do so only because of his generous mail contract. In spite of the efficiency and good name of the C.O.C. and P.P. Exp. Co., it continued to lose money. The hoped-for prize, the overland mail contract, was as far away as ever.

Russell looked to official Washington for aid in getting the contract and was sure he had found it when Senator Gwinn, of California, promised him all his support. Gwinn, who was a strong partisan of the Central Route, was in a position to help bring about a decision very quickly. He was a political figure of great power in Washington, a personal friend of President Buchanan, and also served on the committees that would finally decide the issue.

Gwinn believed that it would take some dramatic demonstration of the superiority of the central route to secure a substantial contract. Although common sense pointed to a choice of a direct, short route, some daring scheme seemed to be in order to convince the powers in Washington once and for all.

Gwinn offered Russell the outline of an incredibly bold plan. It was to run a service, for light mail only, between the Missouri River and California. Men riding the fastest horses in the West would travel in relays, day and night, summer and winter. Four days from the Missouri River to Salt Lake City, and six more to Sacramento would be the time schedule. With an extra few hours for the trip from Sacramento to San Francisco by boat tacked on, it still added up to only half the Butterfield schedule. This lightning service would be the Central Overland Pony Express.

Russell, as always attracted by the new and original, leaped to the suggestion. But the practical Alexander Majors was more cautious than ever since the outcome of the Denver undertaking. He offered a list of arguments against such a wildly fanciful scheme.

[55]

The Pony Express

Majors said the terrible heat of the desert, winter's freezing blizzards, countless outlaws and hostile Indians, all had combined to hamper or destroy every contractor for the mails who had attempted the Central Route. Chorpenning, Hockaday and Liggett, and Kimball's Mormon outfit had all met with complete or partial failure.

Russell's answer to these well-founded arguments was that the Russell, Majors and Waddell outfit was equipped to handle all the problems they would encounter. They had the stations, supply wagons, the mules and oxen, and the work crews to build the new stations and keep the trails open in bad weather. The kind of men they would hire as Pony Expressmen would be able to out-ride the Indians and out-shoot the outlaws. Their horses would be the fastest in the West, the best money could buy. Carefully planned and coordinated, the scheme could not fail.

Russell had all precedent in his favor. From the first, white men in the West had ridden the best horses they could find when they wanted to go somewhere in a hurry. It was the accepted method of fast travel. There had even been a hint of the relay system in the methods of the trappers and traders. As they traveled the early trails, they were never without extra horses if they could help it. Useful as pack animals, the reserve horses could also be used as mounts in case a fast get-away from attacking Indians became necessary. One horse after another might be pushed to his limits and then abandoned along the way.

The West produced celebrated horsemen by the score. Kit Carson, carrying military dispatches out of Bent's Fort on the Santa Fe Trail, set records for long distance trips that were considered amazing, at least until the appearance of Francis Xavier Aubrey. Aubrey was a trader of French-Canadian background, who had his headquarters in Santa Fe. In 1852, he rode from Santa Fe to Independence, Missouri, a distance of 800 miles, in eight days. The next year he accepted a wager of one thousand dollars that he could ride the same distance in less than six days. Although the trip between Santa Fe and Independence had always been a three week journey on horseback, Aubrey was convinced he could win the bet. He had a new idea he was going to put into use. Along the trail horses would be placed here and there so that as his mount tired, a fresh one could be picked up for the next stint.

One September day Aubrey left Santa Fe for the trip east. As he left his starting point farther and farther behind, he found his relay system was completely inadequate. He could have used many times the horses he found waiting for him. Luckily, Santa Fe-bound emigrants he met along the way had heard of Aubrey and his prowess in the saddle and were willing to help him out. Several times he exchanged horses with members of emigrant trains before he finally arrived in Independence. Aubrey had exerted himself to such an extent that he was overcome by exhaustion and had to be lifted from his saddle. But he had finished the race in five and one-half days—an incredible feat.

It may have been Aubrey's accomplishment that gave Senator Gwinn the idea of a continent-spanning Pony Express. At any rate he had convinced Mr. Russell that his idea was a brilliant one. In return Russell had pledged his word that his firm would go along with it if they could count on Gwinn to prod official Washington into action in behalf of a sizable mail contract.

Once more Alexander Majors let himself be persuaded to enter into one of Russell's ventures. The knowledge that Russell had made promises to Gwinn no doubt played a part in influencing the upright Alexander Majors, who felt bound by any commitments made by his partner.

But even greater weight was carried by Senator Gwinn's assurances that the scheme was certain to bring forth the substantial contract needed if the firm of Russell, Majors and Waddell was to operate at a profit. Certain that all factors were working in its behalf, the company now staked everything on the great gamble of the Pony Express.

Russell, Majors and Waddell could not have had a better background for the unprecedented job before it.

As fast as settlements and forts had gone up on the western frontiers, freighting companies appeared to cater to their needs. And Russell, Majors and Waddell was the greatest of them all.

For years their heavy freight wagons had rolled westward, carrying everything from household goods to lumber and machinery, out to the isolated mining camps and homesteads along the trails.

When war with the Mormons threatened, it was Russell, Majors and Waddell who hauled supplies to General Johnston's army, marooned in Utah. An almost endless stream of wagons left their depots in Leavenworth and Nebraska City on the Missouri loaded with food and ammunition for the men at Fort Bridger.

The Bold Plan

[57]

The Pony Express

In 1858, two years before the Pony Express started, the company owned over 6,000 wagons and 75,000 oxen and employed thousands of men. Their superintendents, stationed through the West, ran the firm's activities with admirable discipline and efficiency. All these experienced stage men, Ben Ficklin, John Scudder, Bolivar Roberts, Jim Bromley and many others were called upon immediately to help in the truly colossal job of organizing the Pony Express.

Between the Missouri River and Salt Lake City, their long-established stage and freighting stops were soon put to new use as stations for the Pony. Along this part of the route new intermediate stations shortened the distance between relay points to twenty or twenty-five miles.

FREIGHTING WAGONS

There was a definite system used in transporting heavy freight across the plains. The huge wagons, which carried up to seven thousand pounds of freight, traveled in trains of twenty-five. At their head was a wagon-master or captain, and under the captain an assistant wagon-master, a night herder and bullwhackers, one for each wagon. The captain ruled with an iron hand, bossing the bullwhackers and assigning extra duties as he wished. A bullwhacker could steer the oxen, or bulls, from the tongue of the wagon, but usually he walked beside them, driving them forward with a long whip made of plaited buckskin.

Beyond Salt Lake City the company entered completely new territory. Shelters and stables had to be built at regular intervals across desert and mountain range. Along the old Chorpenning route west of Great Salt Lake, stations went up at Camp Floyd, Deep Creek and Ruby Valley. Wagons drawn by ox-teams dropped building supplies and work crews at Dry Creek, Old River and Bisby's. Adobe, logs, or even stone were used, according to the needs of the area and the materials most easily obtained. A tent would serve now and then, at least temporarily, for a relay stop.

As early as February of 1860, there was talk here and there that Mr. Russell was looking over horses and riders for a fast cross-continent mail service. But the American public in general knew nothing about the diligent planning and organizing going on behind the scenes. From St. Joe to Sacramento, men and boys crowded the company offices when they heard that expert riders were wanted. They came from farms and ranches, isolated settlements and mining camps.

Weeding out the ones who were too heavy or too old, or generally unfitted for the taxing life ahead, was a fairly simple task for the experienced frontiersmen working for Mr. Russell. They were looking for wiry young men, light as jockeys, who would have the endurance to ride fifty miles at top speed. If the trail lay over level ground, twice the distance might be demanded of them.

The rigid rule which insisted upon extreme youth was relaxed at least once during the hiring process. Although most of the men signed on for the Pony were between eighteen and twenty-five, Howard Egan, the famous Mormon pioneer, was past forty when he carried the first Pony mail out of Salt Lake City.

The West of 1860 was a rough and rigorous training ground. Common hardships of everyday living were taken in stride. Strenuous outdoor sports produced exactly the capabilities needed in the men who would make or break the Pony Express. Buffalo still roamed the plains and the buffalo chase was the top pastime of the day. Sometimes the hunter pursued the animal on foot but more often on horseback. He would spur his horse into the herd, taking aim only when he was close upon his prey. Tracking deer or outwitting the dangerous grizzly bear developed initiative and daring that would be useful for a lifetime. Every boy who grew up on the plains or the ranches of California knew

The Bold Plan

[59]

ELK

Deer and elk were everywhere in the West, summering in the Rockies and coming down to the sheltering valleys in winter. Gifted with wonderfully acute hearing, they could confound the hunter with a trick of turning away from the wind when resting. This way they could scent any imminent danger from the rear and at the same time watch for the hunter or preying animals in the opposite direction.

SHOOTING GRIZZLY

A bear hunt was a boy's biggest thrill. The brown or cinnamon grizzly bear was the strongest and most dangerous of animals. Although he looked clumsy and heavy, he moved with lightning speed. The horses were terrified by his powerful roar.

BUFFALO HUNT

Nature gave the buffalo few ways of protecting himself when chased by the hunters. His eyesight was poor and in contrast to his fierce appearance he was by nature extremely mild. But he knew instinctively that he could often unseat his pursuers by fleeing over rough and broken ground.

CAMPING

The thickets bordering the streams of the West were ideal camping spots when hunting for wild turkey, rabbit or other small game. On these trips young boys learned to use firearms and a compass and to follow a trail without getting lost. Woodcraft was essential to the Pony riders.

The Pony Express

something of the exciting business of breaking wild horses to saddle.

He also knew, of necessity, how to tell a hostile Indian from a friendly one. A lone Indian, encountered on the trail, would never approach a raised rifle unless he was looking for a fight. Indian parties on the move left easily read signs behind them. Tracks of unshod Indian ponies could mean that a hunting party or a band of warring young braves was reconnoitering in the vicinity. But if trailing lodge-poles had left their marks in the earth, an Indian village was on the move and any fear of hostility could be dismissed.

The eighty or so men who were signed up for the Pony were not thinking alone of the salary . . . it ranged from fifty to one hundred and fifty dollars a month, a good salary in those days . . . but also of the honor and fun of being a part of this unusual experiment. Riding for the Pony would be something new and exciting!

INDIAN TROUBLE
A raised rifle would determine whether an Indian's intentions were peaceful or not.

Not one objected when he was asked to sign the following pledge of good behavior:

I hereby swear before the great and living God that during my engagement and while I am an employee of Russell, Majors and Waddell, I will under no circumstances use profane language; that I will not quarrel or fight with other employees

[62]

of the firm, and that I will conduct myself honestly, be faithful to my duties, and so direct my acts as to win the confidence of my employers, so help me God.

This pledge was severe for the time and place, but it had long been required of all Russell, Majors and Waddell employees and with good results. Even harder to live up to than this pledge would be another unwritten rule: Mail first, horse second, and self last.

In California W. W. Finney was given the job of picking horses and stocking the stations and he worked with such zeal that the California *Mercantile Journal* spoke of him as "that energetic gentleman." He chose horses for the stamina and sure-footedness needed on dangerous mountain trails. If they were temperamental or half wild, so much the better. High spirits would carry them through situations that no gentle

The Bold Plan

WILD HORSES
The mustangs that roamed in herds over the grassy plains had for ancestors the first horses ever imported into North America—the runaways from ranches as far South as Mexico.

[63]

The Pony Express

horse could face. It might take half a day to shoe a mean California mustang, but the station men were old hands at it. Knowing how to handle any kind of horse was the most important part of the station tender's job. Most of them had had their training handling the firm's cantankerous mules.

At the eastern end of the trail, thoroughbreds from the ranches and cavalry mounts from the military forts at Leavenworth and Kearney helped make up the herd assembled by the spring of 1860. Handpicked, they were the best to be had, since Mr. Russell's agents were permitted to pay three or four times the price of the ordinary horse.

MUSTANG ROUNDUP
Wild horses, when caught and tamed, made the most useful mounts on the plains. Indians had been riding these mustangs for many years when the first white men went into the West. Crossed with better horses, they produced a tireless, rugged half-breed, perfectly suited to traveling long distances without rest.

The famous St. Joseph saddlery run by Israel Landis made a specially designed saddle and mochila under the direction of Bill Cates, who was one of the newly hired riders. The efficient, lightweight saddle shows how thoroughly the needs of the Pony were understood. The mochila was a square leather blanket, with a hard leather mail pocket or box sewn on each corner. It fitted securely over the saddle horn but it could be removed from one saddle and placed on another in a matter of seconds. Once in the saddle, the rider's legs came between the front and rear cantinas, or pockets. Altogether the Pony saddle, including the mochila, weighed about one-third as much as the ordinary Western saddle. The letters and dispatches would be written on thin paper so that up to twenty pounds of mail could be carried and this at five dollars a half ounce. This was a $3200 per horse payload, if the cantinas were full.

Russell's managers outdid themselves when they loaded portable equipment upon the newly hired youths. Certainly no Expressman ever carried all the equipment at one time . . . or at least very far. It included a Bible, a pair of Colt revolvers, a sheath knife and a Spencer carbine. Also a bulky horn with which to alert the station keeper of his approach! All this weight, with the exception of the revolver, was abandoned early in the game. No horn could ever equal the hoofbeats of the pony itself.

As more ads and editorial comment reached the public, interest turned into enthusiasm. Easterners unhesitatingly called the project a noble and praiseworthy undertaking. Settlers living beyond the Missouri and in California were more skeptical of its success. For most of them had learned the risks of the trail at first hand. Few believed that lone horsemen could actually carry the mail two thousand miles in nine days. Memories of floods, sand-storms and blizzards had left them with impressions that were hard to erase.

Beyond Julesburg the Pony route would go directly through the hunting grounds of many Indian tribes that were constantly at war with each other, and spasmodically with white men. The Paiutes in Nevada would certainly consider this a new affront.

On the other hand, if the speedy mail service did work out, eleven days would be cut from any delivery schedule the public had known previously. It was worth trying, and it was earnestly hoped the scheme

The Bold Plan

would materialize. Newspapers urged wholehearted support of the Pony.

To orthodox publicity, Mr. Russell added at least one new method of advertising his new venture. For days before the start, youths wearing bright red shirts and blue trousers were seen in the busy streets of St. Joseph. They appeared in full costume when they attended the dances at Pattee House, the elegant new hotel.

The Pony

Express

By March preparations were so far advanced that advertisements began to appear in leading newspapers throughout the country. The Evening Bulletin of San Francisco printed this ad.

Gus Cliff, Henry Wallace, Alex Carlisle and Billy Richardson were among the Pony men who were looked upon with envy and admiration. The well-known horseman, Johnny Frey, came into town from Rushville to lend a little color to the occasion. St. Joe, a thriving, progress-conscious town was proud to be the starting point of this daring race with time. It was said that the city fathers had even contributed free land in order to attract the Pony to the town.

Little time remained to wonder whether the Pony would be able to carry through, for by late March riders had been quartered along the route, and in stations across two thousand miles men and horses awaited the start of the giant relay.

The Bold Plan

Each letter carried by the Pony Express was written on tissue-thin paper and enclosed in a ten-cent government envelope.

CHAPTER 5

THE BIG DAY

APRIL 3rd fell on Tuesday, but all St. Joseph took a holiday. In the early afternoon the streets were crowded with townspeople and visitors who had come in for the day's festivities. Lots had been drawn for the honor of being the first rider out of St. Joe, and Billy Richardson had come up with the lucky assignment. To his showy red and blue costume he had added ornate boots and gloves. Their fancy decoration of silver and embroidery was repeated in the ornamentation on his pony's saddle and bridle.

[69]

The Pony Express

Both rider and his handsome bay mare were gazed upon with delight by the excited crowd. In fact the people were so pleased by the little horse that she had a hard time keeping her mane or tail intact. Souvenir lockets and bracelets containing hair from the mane and tail of the first Express pony turned up for months in St. Joe.

Music blared from the bunting-draped bandstand, and between tunes important people made speeches, pointing out that this was an historic occasion. Mayor Jeff Thompson's prediction of glorious success called forth showers of applause. Mr. Russell and Mr. Majors were there to enjoy the whole show.

Speeches had been finished and the band had resorted to repeating the same tunes over and over when word arrived by telegraph that the train from Hannibal, on the Mississippi, was going to be late. The Hannibal and St. Joseph railroad, which ran straight across Missouri from East to West, and which was an object of such great pride, was letting them down. The bay mare was put back in her stall at the Pike's Peak Stable, the crowd grew restless and the band played louder and louder. Who would have dreamed that it would be a man-made machine, fashioned for speed, that would give the Pony its first setback? The irony of it was hard to miss.

Later, the New York *Sun* carried this amusing story of the hair-raising train trip from the Mississippi to the Missouri on that spring day in 1860:

The mail car used on the run of the Pony Express was the first car constructed for mail purposes in the United States. The engine, named the Missouri, was a wood burner. From an artistic standpoint it was a much handsomer machine than the big black Moguls of today. There was scrollwork about the headlight, bill and drivers, and all the steel and brass parts were polished till they resembled a looking-glass.

Fuel agents all along the line were notified to be on hand with an adequate force to load the tender in less than no time. The orders given to Engineer Clark were simple. He was to make a speed record to stand for fifty years.

The train pulled out of Hannibal amid the waving of hats and the cheering of a big crowd. All the way across the state, at every station and crossroad it was greeted by enthusiasts, many of whom had journeyed miles to see it. Nothing in Northern Missouri had ever excited greater interest.

The first seventy miles of the journey were comparatively level and straight. Through Monroe and Shelby Counties the eager railway officials figured that the little train was making over sixty miles an hour. At Macon it began to strike the rough country, where hills and curves were numerous.

It stopped at Macon for wood. The fuel agent, L. S. Coleman, had erected a platform, just the height of the tender. On this spot he put every man that could find room, each bearing an armful of selected wood. As the train slowed up, the men emptied their arms. The fuel agent, watch in hand, counted the seconds. Just fifteen seconds passed while the train was at a standstill. Then it was off again, like the wind. The spectators saw the occupants of the car clutching their seats with both hands as it rocked to and fro and threatened to toss them all in a heap on the floor.

Out at Macon at that time was a steep grade running down to the Chariton River. If Clark shut off his steam ever so little on that stretch, none of those on board recollect anything about it. If the man at the throttle were alive today he could look with grim satisfaction at the record he made down that hill. That part of the run, at least, has never been beaten by any engineer who has been in the Company's employ.

It was like an avalanche. If there had been a tenderfoot on board, a more than reasonable doubt would have arisen in his mind as to whether all the wheels of the train were on the track or not. The furnace was drawing magnificently. A streak of fire shot out of the stack, and the wood sparks flew through the air like snowflakes.

Across the Chariton River came the New Cambria Hill, a still greater grade than that down from Macon. The momentum attained served to drive the train halfway up with scarcely any perceptible reduction in speed, but the exhausts became slower before the peak of the grade was approached. The fireman piled his dry cottonwood, and the safety valve sent a column of steam heavenward. The white-faced passen-

The
Big Day

The Pony Express

gers breathed easier, but the relief did not last long. The summit of the hill was reached and the little engine snorted as something alive, took the bit in its teeth, and was soon rushing along at top speed.

While the crowd at St. Joseph waited for the train, preparations were being made at the other end of the route in San Francisco to give the first West-to-East rider a suitable send-off later the same day.

A little yellow pony tied outside the Alta Telegraph office in San Francisco got all the attention he would have received had he been a genuine member of the much-talked-about string of Express ponies. All that was asked of him, actually, was that he walk from the Telegraph office to a sidewheeler that would carry him comfortably up the Sacramento River that night and just as calmly down again the next day. For the yellow pony, charming as he may have been in his gay little flags, was only part of a show put on to dramatize the departure of the mail.

The friendly San Francisco *Bulletin* described it this way:

> From one o'clock until the hour of our going to press, a clean-limbed, hardy little nankeen-colored pony stood at the door of the Alta Telegraph Company's office—the pioneer pony of the famous express which today begins its first trip across the continent. . . . At a ¼ to 4 he takes up his line of march to the Sacramento boat. Personally, he will make short work and probably be back tonight; but by proxy he will put the West behind his heels like a very Puck, and be in New York in thirteen days from this writing.

The rider, James Randall, was a stand-in hired for the afternoon. The demands on him, too, were small, and with good reason, since, according to news stories of the following day, he mounted his horse from the wrong side.

San Franciscans were more than willing to give the Pony a rousing send-off. They could hope to see him only once more at best. If the entire chain of wonderfully synchronized relays came off as hoped, he would be back in ten days. After that the mail made up at the Alta Telegraph office would go to the boat by ordinary messenger. For in those days all traffic—freight, passenger or mail—moved by water from San Francisco to Sacramento.

RIVERBOAT TO SACRAMENTO

CHAPTER 6

ST. JOSEPH TO SAN FRANCISCO

It was already dusk in St. Joseph when a booming cannon announced to the weary crowd that the train had finally arrived. The mail was rushed to the waiting mochila, wrapped in oil silk and locked into the cantinas.

Billy Richardson galloped his horse down Jule Street to the Missouri River, where the ferryboat *Denver* was ready to go. Captain Blackinstone was anxious not to delay the start of the Pony Express by so much as a minute and as soon as Richardson clattered up the gangplank

The Pony Express

the paddle wheels began to turn and the steamboat left the wharf behind.

A little way out from the shore, Richardson had a chance to remove the flashy garb he had worn for the amusement of the crowds in St. Joseph. In its place he put on a frontier hunting shirt made of skins and exchanged his fancy boots and hat for old ones that he had worn on many a long ride before that day. These would be much more comfortable in the tense hours ahead. Richardson knew that as soon as he reached the opposite shore he would have to ride forty miles over black, muddy roads before turning the mochila over to Don Rising, the next courier toward the West.

At Elwood, on the Kansas shore, another crowd stood watching the ferry puff and churn its way across the river. There had been much speculation as to why the Pony Express rider should be late on this very first day of the great mail service. But all the annoyance at being kept waiting changed to enthusiasm when the ferryboat started to swing into place at the Elwood docks.

Across the river the town of St. Joseph could still be seen in the early dusk as the *Denver* tied up and Billy Richardson hurried his mount off the boat. Without pausing to enjoy the hearty cheers that greeted him, he urged his horse through the streets and turned toward the open prairies that stretched westward from the Missouri.

ST. JOSEPH FROM ACROSS THE RIVER

The trails west had never known such speed. Out along the winding road that led to Granada, Richardson's last stop, homesteaders who had heard the talk about the fast mail, waited anxiously to see the first Pony dash by. Way stations at Cold Springs, Troy, Lancaster and Kennekuk stood ready to give Billy Richardson a helping hand. At each stop the mochila was swept from the back of the in coming horse and fitted quickly into place upon another, already saddled, bridled and prancing to go. Safely locked away in the cantinas were forty-nine letters, five telegrams and a few copies of the St. Joseph *Daily Gazette,* all destined for the military posts and larger towns, hundreds of miles to the west.

Four times the mochila was slapped on a fresh mount before Richardson began the last lap to Granada. Everything had come off without a hitch. The right horses had been ready in the right spots and the excited station keepers eager to see that not a second was lost.

The Pony had got a late start out of St. Joe but Richardson had already made up a good forty-five minutes of the time lost, when he galloped into Granada, where the impatient Don Rising was waiting to take over.

Riding out of Granada Don Rising took to the old military road that ran west from Fort Leavenworth. The road ran straight across the Kickapoo Indian reservation and Rising settled down to a steady pace that would put the miles behind him. The Kickapoos had hardly been mentioned when arguments against starting the Pony had been brought up. They were friendly Indians who stayed put in their villages, raising their crops of corn and beans and pumpkins. The Pony riders would never have any trouble with them.

Beyond Log Chain Station, Rising rode across rolling prairie to Seneca, an important point for the Pony Express and also for the Overland stage coaches. The modest Smith's Hotel, where they both stopped briefly, seemed bigger and more luxurious than it really was, only because it was the only inn of any description between St. Joseph and Marysville, Kansas. Every noted person who made the trip east or west, stopped at Smith's Hotel. Jim Bridger, the famous scout and trapper, William G. Fargo of the Wells Fargo Express Company, Senators and newsmen, had all sampled the wonderful hospitality and enjoyed the fine cooking before boarding the stages again.

[77]

St. Joseph to San Francisco

The Pony Express

At Ash Point and Guittard's ranch, Rising stopped for no more than a minute. The tenders waiting with fresh horses barely had time to wish him well and send him on his way. Ten miles farther on, Rising clattered into Marysville, which lay on the Big Blue River. He was lucky to have his home station in such a spot. Marysville was alive with all the hurly-burly of the trail, for it was here that lesser roads from the East joined the Oregon Trail. All the ox-drawn wagons and mule teams headed for the forts out on the plains, passed through Marysville; every stage carrying passengers westward over the Oregon Trail, paused there.

LEAVING MARYSVILLE

In Marysville the Pony Express kept its horses at Cottrell's livery stable. It was here that Jack Keetley began his first ride which ran out across the Blue River and up the Oregon Trail.

There would be more traffic to watch out for, now that the Pony was following the main road to the West. A speeding horse would have to pass around the slow moving emigrant wagons. Back in St. Joseph everyone would be wondering how the Pony was making out and betting for it or against it. Perhaps some east bound traveler would carry the word back that Keetley had been seen moving west at a great rate of speed.

Keetley's home stop was at Cottonwood station on the ranch owned by the Hollenberg family. The long, low frame building not only housed the family but also a general store and post office. The second story

[78]

served as a common bedroom for a half-dozen or more Overland employees, including the Pony rider. These cramped quarters were luxurious by comparison with the ones farther west, where the boys would have to put up with any kind of lodging that could be found.

The early spring morning was well along when Henry Wallace took charge of the mochila just arrived from the east and began his run up the Little Blue River. This was the most beautiful part of the entire trail. Through dense, dark woodlands the Little Blue wound its way, until near its upper reaches, the thinning forests gave notice that the Platte country was nearing. Prairie grasslands gave way to sagebrush

St. Joseph to San Francisco

ALONG THE TRAIL

The Pony Express

country. A little farther on, a tree had become rare enough to serve as a landmark. Two hundred miles from the Missouri river, a way station had been put up in the vicinity of a solitary tree and had been given the plainly appropriate name of Lone Tree station.

For nearly seven hundred miles the trail would follow the Platte or its branches. Flooding extravagantly in the spring and all but disappearing in the heat of summer, the Platte was still the most important river of the plains. Sometimes the trail lay beside the broad river. At other times sandhills, gullied by heavy rains and polished by wind, forced the trail far back from the river banks.

The grade of the Platte valley inclined more and more upward, the country became increasingly dry and treeless. Stations were a little closer together, now that the ranch country had been left behind.

FORT KEARNEY

The first thing the rider saw when approaching Fort Kearney was the Stars and Stripes waving in the breeze and after that the trees which had been planted in the early days of the Fort and carefully tended ever since. They appeared very beautiful after a long ride across treeless country. Fort Kearney was the oldest army post on the Oregon Trail. It had been built the year before the gold rush to California had begun, and ever since had been a spot that emigrants on the trail looked forward to with pleasure.

It was a fine place to buy supplies and get information, and the best place from which to mail a letter back east. The Pony rider heading west from Fort Kearney rode into the beginning of the buffalo country.

FORT KEARNEY POST OFFICE

Near Plum Creek, his home station, there was a place on the Platte where the buffalo liked to come to drink. The boys carrying the mail between Fort Kearney and Julesburg would have buffalo steak to eat instead of bacon and beans. The ones riding the other side of the South Pass would have it harder. All provisions there had to be brought in by wagon. And the prices soared so that a Pony rider could not afford to eat, except that Mr. Russell was paying for it, no matter how much it cost. A dish of meat and potatoes might cost a dollar and a half, and a piece of pie sometimes sold for a dollar.

Many tribes of Plains Indians camped along the Platte. At a distance their lodges looked like paper cones set down on the plains. As you came nearer you could see that they were made of buffalo hides, sewn together and stretched tight over a framework of light poles. The Indians knew where to camp to make living easy, and they liked to hunt antelope as well as buffalo. When the hunting was found to be poor,

[8 1]

The Pony Express

an Indian village could pack up everything, including the tepees, in a couple of hours and move on to more promising territory.

About a hundred miles west of Fort Kearney was Cottonwood Springs, one of the more comfortable home stations. Long before anyone had dreamed of the Pony Express, emigrants had used this point on the trail as a camping ground. The cedar trees which filled the canyons made the spot cool and inviting, and also furnished fuel needed for cooking. Since 1858, Cottonwood Springs had had a stage station, a store and warehouse and stables for the horses. Unlike the relay stations, where only a couple of men were in charge, the home stations usually had a crew of highly skilled tenders and blacksmiths. It took two to handle the kind of horse the Pony riders used. Two to rope the animal, and then one to sit on his head while the blacksmith busied himself around the unwilling hooves.

The rush to Pike's Peak was in full swing again, after a cold, long winter, and around Fremont Springs, the Pony rider had to exercise great caution in order not to run headlong into an emigrant train on its way to Denver.

Eleven fast miles lay between Elkhorn and O'Fallon's Bluff. The rugged, wild country around O'Fallon's was an ideal spot for Indians to lurk and attack from ambush. Fourteen miles remained to be cov-

INDIAN AMBUSH

[82]

ered before coming to Alkali Lake, and twenty more to Diamond Springs, where the canyon walls were so high and sheer that the stage boys called the spot Devil's Dive. At Julesburg, a rude settlement of unpainted shacks, the Pony forded the Platte and turned northwest up

St. Joseph to San Francisco

CHIMNEY ROCK IN THE DISTANCE

Lodgepole Creek. The route now struck across a sandy ridge to the North Platte and a region weird with strange rock formations.

When the tall spire of Chimney Rock was seen in the distance, it meant the Pony was coming into the mountain region.

On across the plains the Pony sped, methodically ticking off the miles.

ACROSS THE PLAINS

[8 3]

The Pony Express

CHEESE CREEK STATION

Out in western Nebraska a homesteader living along the trail, was glad to earn a little money by providing a stop for the Pony rider.

PRAIRIE DOG VILLAGE

The trail curved to pass by a village of prairie dogs and the noise of their barking rose from a thousand mounds. It was spring and the dogs had come out of their burrows to nibble the fresh, tender grasses.

[84]

FORT LARAMIE

On a sandy spit of land between the Platte and Laramie rivers, stood Fort Laramie, the busiest point on the trail. Paths worn down by generations of Crows, Cheyennes and Arapahoes radiated over the plains and mountains. The Fort was in the heart of the Indian hunting grounds and inside there were Indians everywhere, trading their furs for food and guns, looking the emigrants over, killing time in a lively place.

BUFFALO HERD

Bullwhackers, trappers and soldiers mingled with tenderfoot emigrants from the East.

Leaving Fort Laramie, the Pony pushed on up the Platte toward the valley of the Sweetwater. Riders in this area would have to watch out for roving buffalo herds. The boys on the night runs would just have to trust to luck that they did not gallop right into the middle of one.

[85]

The Pony Express

In the foothill country around Horseshoe Creek, the hills were steep and the going underfoot was rough. The route now crossed the North Platte, and continued on to the point where the great pile of gray granite called Independence Rock stood alone on the plain.

DEVIL'S GATE

Farther on a few miles and the Pony rounded Devil's Gate, a huge cleft in the granite ridge through which the Sweetwater flows.

Following the narrow valley the trail led to the foothills of the Rockies where the wide grassy valley of South Pass offered an easy crossing to the western slopes. Long before the westward emigration had begun, this gap in the mountains had been discovered by the mountain men who got to know every hill and valley, in their wanderings over the west in search of skins.

St. Joseph
to San
Francisco

THREE CROSSING STATION

At Three Crossing station, on the Sweetwater, the station men waved the Pony rider on his way over South Pass.

The most famous of all the trappers and scouts was Jim Bridger, who knew the country and the Indians backwards and forwards. It was on the site of his old trading post that the government had established a military fort two years before. Fort Bridger was a small and unimpressive post, garrisoned by only two or three companies of soldiers.

Southwest of Fort Bridger and all through Utah, most of the Pony Express riders were Mormon boys. Thomas Owen King was one of this hard riding crew, and it was he who carried the mail for the first time from Fort Bridger to Echo Canyon. At the mouth of the canyon stood Hanks Station, an oasis in the barren country, walled in by brown,

[87]

The Pony Express

perpendicular mountains. It was Echo Canyon that Brigham Young and the early Mormons had traversed on their journey to the Great Salt Lake.

It was into Brigham Young's well ordered and thriving Salt Lake City that a tired Pony expressman galloped on the evening of April 9th, bringing the first mail from the east.

Since the mail which had left Sacramento on April 3rd had already arrived, the Pony Express was already a proven success so far as resi-

SALT LAKE CITY

dents of Salt Lake City were concerned. News from Washington would now be only seven days old, and letters from the Missouri frontier would come inside of six days. To people used to a lag of two or three months in their mail delivery, this was an almost unbelievable blessing. At the Pony headquarters on State Street, enthusiasm over the Pony's arrival was doubled by the knowledge that the doubters and pessimists had been shown to be wrong.

[88]

The *Deseret News* of Salt Lake City published an editorial praising the backers of the Express:

St. Joseph
to San
Francisco

The Pony Express: The first Pony Express from the West left Sacramento City at 12 p.m. on the night of the 3rd inst. and arrived in this city at 11:45 p.m. of the 7th, inside of prospectus time. The roads were heavy and the weather stormy. The last 75 miles was made in 5 hours, 15 minutes in a heavy rain.

The Express from the East left St. Joseph, Missouri, at 6:30 p.m. on the evening of the 3rd and arrived in this city at 6:25 p.m. on the evening of the 9th. The difference in time between this city and St. Joseph is something near 1 hour and 15 minutes, bringing us within six days' communication with the frontier, and seven days from Washington—a result which we Utahians, accustomed to receive news three months after date, can well appreciate.

Much credit is due the enterprising and persevering originators of this enterprise and, although a telegraph is very desirable, we feel well satisfied with this achievement for the present.

The weather has been disagreeable and stormy for the past week and in every way calculated to retard the operations of the company, and we are informed the Express eastward from this place was five hours in going to Snyder's Mill, a distance of 25 miles.

We are indebted to Mr. W. H. Russell for a copy of the St. Joseph *Daily Gazette,* printed expressly for Utah and California, with dates from Washington and New York to the evening of the 2d, and from St. Joseph to 6 p.m. of the 3d inst.

The probability is, the Express will be a little behind time in reaching Sacramento this trip, but when the weather becomes settled, and the roads good, we have no doubt they will be able to make the trip in less than ten days.

The boys who kept the relay going through Utah and Nevada rode through the weirdest part of the West. From the red and gray sagebrush flats of Utah, a labyrinth of barren mountain ridges stretched west-

The Pony Express

ward, broken and bewildering. For five hundred miles between Camp Floyd and Carson City, there were almost no white men except the Pony tenders spotted along the way. An adobe shelter was a luxury in this arid land of alkali and salt flats. There had been no clear cut choice to be made when the Pony route was established through the Great Salt Lake Basin. No safest and best route existed. Some paths led through country which was completely dry most of the year. Other sections, with more oases to their credit, were impassable during the snowy season.

Occasionally the rider would pass an Indian village, but this was no comfort to him since the attitude of the Indians was an unknown quantity.

INDIAN VILLAGE

The trail finally chosen lay a little south of the one followed by the Forty-niners. In general it took the old, much-traveled Chorpenning route. It ran by way of Simpson's Springs and Fish Springs.

Farther west, almost on the border of Utah and Nevada, was Deep Creek Station, its low buildings standing alone against the sky. Up steep mountains and down gravelly canyons, the Pony raced on his way to Carson City. At Egan Canyon and Butte Valley only the station men who had been placed there so recently said hello and goodbye to the hurried rider.

[90]

St. Joseph to San Francisco

CARSON CITY

Carson City itself had a very misleading name, for the title of city was a great exaggeration. A tiny, insignificant town, it was still the only true settlement within hundreds of miles. And the Cottonwood trees lining the banks of the Carson River were the only trees any rider had seen in a thousand miles.

On the afternoon of April 12, Warren Upson, who had proved the Pony Express a success by his eastward ride over the mountains, began his first return trip to Sportsman's Hall. The snow was no longer falling, and the trail was crowded with wagons lumbering along with supplies for the new mines in Nevada. Again and again he was forced to leave the road and ride around the outfits which blocked his way. Bill Hamilton was on hand at Sportsman's Hall, set to carry on down to Sacramento.

The Pony Express

PLACERVILLE

At Placerville·Hamilton was forced to lose a few minutes when he was escorted out of town by the Mayor and a cheering mob. He did not want the same thing to happen in Sacramento, but he was not prepared for the excitement in store for him upon his arrival there.

WELCOME TO SACRAMENTO

A group of horsemen met him at Sutter's Fort and rode with him into town. Men, women and children jammed the sidewalks and hung from windows and balconies to watch the new hero race through the town. Every church bell was pealing and cannon in the square boomed a nine-gun salute as the rider appeared at the head of J Street. The horsemen racing beside him created so much confusion and raised so much dust that Hamilton could hardly find his way to the docks.

[92]

BOAT FROM SACRAMENTO

On the river the sidewheeler *Antelope* was waiting to carry him down to San Francisco.

SAN FRANCISCO AT LAST!

In the future San Franciscans would get their mail in an ordinary mail bag, but they were ready to make the most of their one visit from the Pony. Bands were playing when the *Antelope* swung in to the docks, and Bill Hamilton's horse walked off the boat to the strains of "See, the Conquering Hero Comes." Torchlights and bonfires turned the night into day as an excited procession began its tour of the crowded streets.

[93]

Highly polished fire engines led the way and the Pony followed, stepping proudly beneath the flapping flags and banners. Behind the Pony and his rider milled the excited crowd, on foot and in carriages. One woman tore the ribbons from her bonnet and tied them around the Pony's neck. Till far into the morning the celebration continued and

SAN FRANCISCO

San Franciscans went home to bed happy in the knowledge that from now on the Pony would keep them in touch with the important happenings in the East. From now on the East would know that San Francisco was on the way to becoming one of the nation's leading cities.

CELEBRATES

CHAPTER 7

TROUBLE ON THE TRAIL

IN THE early days of the West, white men usually looked upon the Indian as a friend. The trappers and traders who first explored the streams and mountain passes of the western ranges lived close to the red man, often growing to think and act as he did. Often they even shared the Indian's superstitions.

It was to the advantage of both Indian and mountain man, and their mutually pleasant business relationship, that they keep enmity out of the picture as much as possible. To the white man the Indian brought

The Pony Express

skins and furs, destined for the fashionable trade back East. In return he received blankets and guns and whiskey, and all the cheap, factory-made household goods and trinkets he could use.

Indians could understand men who were nomads like themselves. These small numbers of white men came for furs and when they had got them, went away again. There was plenty of room for all and it was easy to see that they did not want to take over the land.

This happy state of affairs ended abruptly when the Forty-Niners invaded the West. Indians watched helplessly as swarms of white men traversed the trails through their hunting grounds, cutting down the timber and killing off the game. Before long fearful tales of Indian attacks began to be heard along the trail. Wagons traveling alone or in small groups, it was said, would almost always be attacked from ambush and emigrants killed and scalped. Stories of kidnapings and torture were told and retold until they grew to nightmare proportions. Acting out of fear, the emigrant often shot at a friendly Indian, thus bringing disaster upon himself

As the fur trade petered out and emigrants continued to pour into the West, relations between the red man and white became more and more dangerous. As early as 1850 it seemed advisable for the U. S. Government to arrange some kind of agreement between the two races. Word was sent out to all the different tribes that a great council was to be held the following year.

In the summer of 1851, Indians by the score began to put up their tepees in the area around Horse Creek, near Fort Laramie. From the Arkansas river all the way north to the Canadian border, the tribes sent their representatives, many of them coming from great distances with wives and children in tow. Shoshone, Cheyenne, Arapaho, Assiniboine, Crow, Mandan, and Aricara gathered ten-thousand strong to find out what the white men would say about the boundaries of their hunting grounds.

Jim Bridger, who had lived with Indians for many years, was on hand to aid in the negotiations, along with Thomas Fitzpatrick, the trapper and Indian agent. All the way from

TRAPPER
Trappers sometimes adorned themselves with feathers and skins as lavishly as possible.

Washington came D. D. Mitchell, the superintendent of Indian affairs. The Indian chiefs put on their most ornamental feathers and brightest paint for the occasion. For a while they forgot their old tribal hostilities and smoked a peace pipe together. Everyone, including the children, was on his best behavior.

The squaws built a large pavilion to be used as a meeting place and on September 8th, 1851, the deliberations began. Everything went smoothly and the council brought forth the very first treaty between Indian and white man, the beginning of a long series of treaties between the two races. Under its terms the United States government obtained the right to build roads and forts in some parts of Indian territory, without hindrance from the Indians. In return the tribes were to receive $50,000 worth of goods every year for fifty years and to have certain hunting grounds left for their use alone.

INDIAN TRAVEL
Women of the Indian tribes were accustomed to doing heavy labor. When moving day came, they did most of the packing and loading and might then walk long distances to the next campsite.

The wagon train carrying the first load of presents was known to be on its way across the plains, but had not arrived when the council ended. But the Indians waited patiently and the goods were distributed in an atmosphere of good will.

The Pony Express

Back in Washington, however, the current policy of thrift before anything else, soon brought about a change in the terms of the treaty. The fifty-year period of the agreement was cut down to fifteen years and the papers were returned to all the tribes for resigning. All but the Crow Indians assented to the change without question.

The document which had been intended to smooth out the touchy relations between the two races actually helped very little if at all. Much of the goods intended for the Indians never even reached them. Some of it was handled by dishonest agents who had complete control over its distribution and who found this chance of pocketing a little dishonest money far too good to miss. Blankets and warm clothing were sold to traders who in turn sold them to the Indians, who were already the rightful owners. By way of appeasing the Indians they were loaded with cheap jewelry and bad whiskey, sometimes manufactured especially for them.

HUNTING BUFFALO
To the Plains Indian hunting was a duty to be performed, a way of getting the necessary meat and skins. Warfare was his real life and joy.

The complete inability of the white man to keep the treaties he made with the Indians was one of the reasons for the Indian's growing hostility. Another cause was the senseless slaughtering of the buffalo, the animal around which the life of the Plains Indian revolved.

For most Indians the buffalo was the source of all things physical and spiritual. Indian legends and religious ceremonies had their beginning in the stories told about the buffalo migrations and the yearly hunt.

The Indian did not waste any part of the buffalo carcass. While the emigrant killed them for the hump, or even the tongue alone, the Indian utilized every bit of hide, bone and hair. His clothing, tepee, war shields and saddles were made from the hide, which the squaws tanned and sewed. Weapons were made of the larger bones, and rope woven of the hair. His very existence depended on the bison, which had roamed in great herds before the coming of the white man.

Gradually the superstition arose that a buffalo would never return to a spot where he had once smelled a white man.

It was much the same story among the Paiutes of Nevada and Utah. Although they were not buffalo hunters—for there were no buffalo in the grassless desert country—the Paiutes, too, saw their food supply disappearing as the white men started to take over their territory. Every new discovery of silver in the hills of Nevada brought more white men into the area. Antelope, the only game existing in any quantity, steadily became harder to find. The pinon trees which bore the nourishing nuts which the squaws pounded into meal, were rapidly being cut down for building material and for firewood.

By the spring of 1860, when the first Pony Express cut across the plains and mountains, the Paiutes were alarmed and angry at the great numbers of prospectors spreading over the hills. They had always looked upon white people as enemies and from the first had been a menace to wagon trains. This new threat of the Pony Express, represented by a string of stations suddenly built at close intervals, drove them to fury.

PEACEFUL INDIANS
At first, the Paiutes of Nevada took the Pony Express calmly, but their resentment grew.

[101]

St. Joseph to San Francisco

The Pony Express

The Pony had successfully made eight trips, when the full force of the Indians' resentment made itself felt along the Pony trail. One day in May the Pony rider heading for Carson City reined in at Williams station for a change of horse. Instead of the saddled mount he expected to find waiting for him, he found the station a ruin, and the bodies of five men mutilated by Indians. The station keeper himself had escaped death only because he was out hunting. This was just the beginning of depredations which would spread along the trail and stop the Pony altogether for a month.

At Simpson's Park, prospectors on the way to Pike's Peak found the station men murdered. At Dry Creek, rider Thomas Flynn arrived only to learn that the attendants had been killed and the horses stolen. Cowering in terror were six bewildered emigrants, not knowing whether to stay or go on their way. Station men along the route were at the mercy of attacking Indians. In Nevada and Utah it was largely a matter

STATION

At a relay station the Pony rider would change horses and be on his way to the next stop in a few seconds. The station attendants had to stay where they were, no matter how lonely or dangerous the life was.

of luck if they escaped being scalped, for it was only at a few of the more important stops that there were more than two men in charge. This was the case at Egan Canyon station when it was set upon by warring Indians in the spring of 1860.

Henry Wilson was in charge at Egan Canyon station and he had as an assistant, Albert Armstrong, who looked after the horses. Their station was a crude, one-room cabin which offered the barest protection from the weather and from hostile Indians. Wilson and Armstrong were eating breakfast one morning, when blood-curdling yells told them that a long expected attack had come.

They both grabbed rifles and extra ammunition and hit the floor. As they ducked arrows which were whizzing into the room, they poured shots through cracks in the walls until their ammunition was exhausted. This was what the Indians were waiting for. They kicked down the door and burst into the cabin in a new fury over losing several of their band.

Luckily for Wilson and Armstrong, the Indians were ravenously hungry, and the sight of breakfast set out and waiting to be eaten was too much for them. The station men were tied hand and foot but won a short delay of the tortures to come while the Indians gobbled all the food in sight and searched the storeroom for more. The food situation disposed of, the braves brought firewood and sagebrush with the intention of burning the building with the keepers tied up inside.

It was at this moment that the white men heard the hoof beats of horses coming at a gallop. Soldiers sent out from Fort Bridger to patrol the trail had arrived just in time to prevent an Indian victory. Colonel Steptoe's band of twenty soldiers killed eighteen Paiutes in the fight that followed. Some Indians were lucky enough to get away, however, and that night they took some fresh recruits from the tribe and attacked the station at Schell Creek. This time they succeeded in carrying out their plan and killed the men in charge.

Trouble on the Trail

SCALP
The Indian brave who had just taken possession of another scalp, had proven once again that he was a master in his profession, the business of making war.

The Pony Express

For nearly three hundred miles the Pony route was open to Indian attack at any time. Bands of armed warriors waited in concealment to waylay a speeding rider, or rode whooping upon the small isolated stations.

Sometimes when the Pony riders met hostile Indians on the trail, their only defense lay in pulling a bold and daring bluff on the savages. Howard Egan, whose run lay just west of Salt Lake City, had to take a desperate chance one night when he ran into a band of Paiutes. Riding down a steep canyon, Egan saw a light from a campfire shining in the distance. In a few moments he had come to a point from which he could make out the forms of Indians lined up on both sides of the road. He could still turn back and go through another canyon six or

THE RIDERS OFTEN SAW EVIDENCES OF INDIAN

eight miles to the north. But Egan was aware that the Indians knew about that passage, too, and probably had another party posted there.

He quickly decided to brazen it out. Approaching as quietly as possible, Egan suddenly put spurs to his mount, at the same time shouting at the top of his lungs and firing his pistol into the air. He caught a glimpse of Indians scurrying up the banks as he thundered on out of the canyon to safety. The Indians, who had got the impression from all the noise that Egan made that there was a squad of horsemen behind him, lost a few precious minutes while Egan made his getaway.

Later a friendly Indian told Egan that the Paiutes were eager to catch an express rider to see what he carried. According to the Indians it must be unknown magic in the saddle boxes that made him go so fast.

Trouble on the Trail

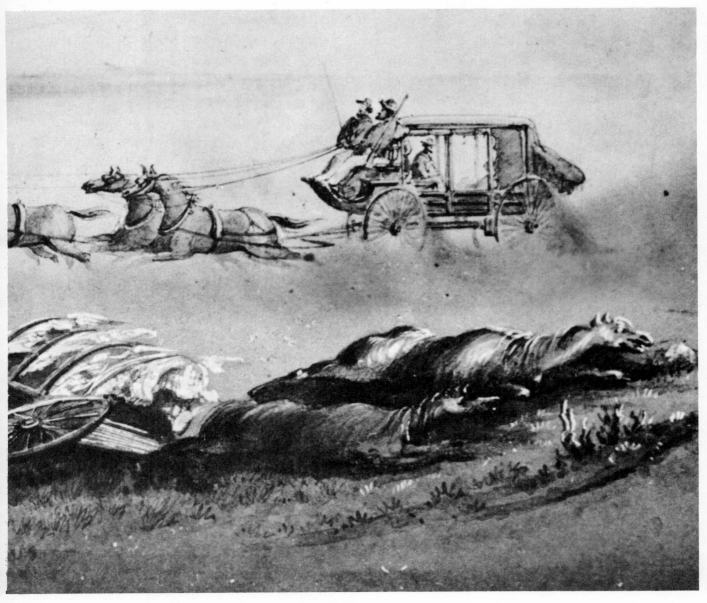

ATTACKS ON WAGON TRAINS ALONG THE WAY

The Pony Express

When it first became apparent that the Pony Express was running into trouble, newspapers in the West, which had begun to rely on the Pony for news dispatches, expressed alarm over losing their source of information. The Sacramento *Union* had this to say about the interruption:

> Up to the closing of the Alta Telegraph office last night, about half past ten o'clock, nothing was heard of the Pony Express, and we have fears that it has been interrupted by the Indian difficulties. Such a result will be much regretted by all the people of the state, who have just begun to appreciate the blessing of a ready transmission of intelligence from the East.

Other papers called for military protection for the riders, lest the Pony be stopped altogether. Indian raids continued, with burnings and lootings of the stations now expected at any time. Settlers who had scattered over the mining country in Nevada, went into Virginia City and Carson City for protection.

From the two towns a body of men organized to go into the hills and punish the Paiutes. Major Ormsby headed a force of over a hundred men who set off one morning on an expedition they all considered a lark. Somewhere near Pyramid Lake, Indians were seen for a moment but soon disappeared. The careless volunteers, pursuing the Paiutes into strange territory, rode directly into an Indian ambush, well planned and carried out.

Suddenly at a sign from the leader, Indians appeared from behind every bush and hillock, pouring fire upon the white men. Major Ormsby was among the first to be wounded and the disorganized band panicked and fled, the Indians close on their heels. The retreat was complete chaos, and only half of the men ever got to safety.

The disaster at Pyramid Lake had one good result. It brought about the establishment of semi-military groups in the towns, and brought into the picture a force of United States troops, who chased the Paiutes deep into the mountains. After this the attacks were far less frequent, but the Pony had by this time been stopped.

The backers of the Pony saw that their chances of being subsidized by the government would be ruined unless they could avoid any more delays in the schedule. They asked for seventy-five soldiers to be placed

along the route between Carson City and Dry Creek, the most dangerous part of the trail. This appeal was denied, but that troops in the
area were of some help is evident from the following news story from
the *Deseret News* of Salt Lake City, on June 20, 1860:

The express from the West which left California 25th May,
arrived Tuesday 19th, at 14 past 10 a.m., and immediately
left for the States. The Indians are still troublesome, annoying the stations in front and rear of the troops. Part of the
troops were stationed at Schell Creek and Ruby Valley, and
the balance went on west with the mail as an escort, in
company with Major Egan. Mr. Morrell, postmaster of this
city, with a company of others, with the mail, had arrived
at Ruby Valley from California, and the mail is expected here
in the course of a few days.

PONY BOB
The exploits of Pony Bob Haslam provided material for many paintings and drawings.

The Pony Express

Small wonder that Bolivar Roberts, who headed the western section, was worried. It had taken over three weeks to bring the mail from Sacramento to Salt Lake City, a distance formerly covered in four or five days. The Indians had trailed the party of men carrying the mail all through Nevada, sometimes destroying the stations before the riders were out of sight.

Immediately, stronger stations of stone or adobe were put up, with safe corrals for the animals. Veritable forts of adobe were built between Carson City and Dry Creek, and extra men put on as guards.

During the Indian trouble, the riders for the Pony Express used every trick known on the frontier to avoid meeting a redskin. Sometimes they cut across country in order to skirt an especially dangerous spot. A creek would be forded at a different point, or a new passage through the hills would be followed, even though it added a few miles

POPULAR HERO
Pony Bob was so popular throughout the West that a colored postcard showing him on one of his famous rides was put on sale.

to the run. At times the rider would dismount before he reached the brow of a hill, scan the country ahead for any danger signals and, if he saw none, go like lightning across the flat terrain where he could easily be seen.

One story of a narrow escape from Indians concerned "Pony Bob" Haslam, and was told over and over along the trail. Haslam had an extremely dangerous run between Friday's station and Buckland's, in Nevada. One day while he was still several miles from his home station, he found his path blocked by armed Paiutes.

As Haslam approached at a gallop, expecting to be shot at any minute, the leader of the band made a peace signal and the way was cleared for him to go through. As Haslam rode away he heard the leader shout, "You pretty good fellow, you go ahead." Perhaps the Indian recognized Haslam, who was a very famous rider, or it may be that on this occasion they were merely curious to have a good look at one of the fast horsemen.

Haslam had many more adventures, and it was he who set a record for endurance that no other rider ever came close to. The carefully worked out routine for the riders had been all but destroyed when Haslam made his famous run from Friday's station to Smith's Creek.

On arriving at Reed's station, just west of Buckland's, he found that some unknown volunteer, gone to fight the Indians, had taken off on the horse he needed to carry him on his next relay. Haslam stopped only long enough to feed his exhausted horse, then forced him on to Buckland's, ordinarily his final stop.

At Buckland's Haslam found the rider too terrified of Indians to go out. He had no choice but to continue on his way. But this time he at least had a fresh pony to carry him the thirty-five miles to the Sink of the Carson. Three more quick changes of horse took him past Cold Springs, Sand Springs and started him on his final thirty-mile run to Smith's Creek, where Jay Kelley was waiting to take over. Haslam had ridden one hundred and eighty-five miles, instead of his regular seventy-five, when he turned the mochila over to a new rider.

Haslam's return trip to Friday's station was a harrowing one even for the bold Pony Bob. After nine hours of sleep, he started out with the mail from the East. At Cold Springs, where he had stopped only a few hours before, all the horror of a recent Indian raid met his eyes. The mutilated body of the station keeper lay near the burned out ruin of the station. As at Reed's station on the previous day, not a horse was in sight. This time they had all been driven off by the Indians. Once again he must urge a tired horse on for an extra run.

It was dark when he reached Sand Springs. When the lone station attendant heard of the raid at Cold Springs, he decided to seek shelter

The Pony Express

in a safer spot. He went with Haslam to the next station to the west, where there would at least be a number of men to keep him company.

Arriving at the Sink of the Carson, they found fifteen men in a state of alarm over a recent encounter with the Indians. They were sure that the station was completely surrounded by a war party and pleaded with Haslam not to risk his life further that night.

After a short rest, however, Haslam went on and arrived at Buckland's only three and a half hours late. His own run to Friday's station still lay before him, but it was made in good time and without incident.

Haslam had covered three hundred and seventy miles within a few hours of the regular schedule, when he rode into Friday's. He had been in great danger every foot of the way, and had expected to be pounced on at every bend in the trail. According to Haslam, it was the excitement that kept him going.

Once in a while a rider had "Indian trouble" which was amusing,

END OF THE TRAIL
Because the riders could out-ride and out-shoot the Indians,
only one of them lost his life at their hands.

at least after it was well in the past. Jay Kelley carried the mail east from Smith's Creek. One day while he was speeding past a slow moving emigrant train, he suddenly realized that he was being shot at repeatedly. On his return trip the following day, he came upon the same string of wagons, and proceeded to give the surprised travelers a good bawling out. Their explanation was a logical one, "We thought you was an Indian." Kelley had been mistaken for an Indian sent out as a decoy. This was not surprising, since the emigrants knew that this method was sometimes used by a band of warriors to draw attention from their own approach.

The Paiute war on the Pony Express lasted only a few weeks, but cost the company the lives of many men and about $75,000 in stations and livestock lost to the Indians. When the courier service was made semi-weekly in the summer of 1860 the public cheered, but behind the scenes there was already much concern over the future of the Pony.

Trouble on the Trail

CHAPTER 8

STORM CLOUDS IN THE EAST

CHRISTMAS WEEK of 1860 saw the beginning of a political scandal that shocked the nation and dealt the Pony Express a blow from which it never recovered. Three million dollars worth of bonds from the Indian Tribal Fund were reported missing, and along with them had disappeared Godard Bailey, a clerk in the Department of the Interior.

The same day, William H. Russell, the organizing genius of the Pony Express, was arrested in his offices on Fulton Street, New York City. He was accused of receiving the bonds from Bailey and using

The Pony Express

them for security in obtaining a huge loan. In their place had been left "acceptances" issued earlier by Secretary of War Floyd, to Russell, Majors and Waddell, for freighting contracts.

Russell's bail was set at two hundred thousand dollars. In no time at all friends and admirers had raised over two million, and Russell left prison to appear before a special Congressional committee. No record of his testimony is in existence, but the committee's report denounced the Secretary of the Interior for negligence and spoke of Russell's answers as incomplete and evasive.

As was to be expected, Russell was completely unable to make restitution for the missing bonds. Much later, however, Congress was to pass an act authorizing reimbursement to the Indian Tribal Fund. Although Russell insisted that he did not know the bonds were stolen when he accepted them, the bad publicity had totally destroyed any chance of getting government backing for the Pony Express.

On the other hand it had not injured Russell's personal popularity in the least. He was still the "Napoleon" of the plains, who had amazed the West with the success of his swift and daring Pony Express. When he visited Colorado a few months later, a ball was given in his honor at Golden, Colorado. Public officials, including the Governor, were present to show the world that they believed Russell to be innocent of any intent to defraud.

As the Civil War approached, the Pony gave more and more valuable service to the nation. In spite of debts which were piling up daily, the fleet horses sped back and forth without ceasing between East and West. On November 7th, 1860, telegraph wires in the East were humming with the news that Abraham Lincoln had been elected President of the United States. St. Louis flashed the news to St. Joseph, and it was rushed West by Pony Express.

The government's hold on California at this time was a rather tenuous one. Although they had entered the Union as a free state, there were many Californians who were in sympathy with the South, and hoped to see California join the Confederacy. If this happened, the wealth of the Gold State might turn the tide of war. Plots to turn the state over to the South had been uncovered. One such group, the Knights of the Golden Circle, had made plans for forming an independent nation on the Pacific coast before joining the Confederacy.

The period between Lincoln's election and his inauguration in March was a critical one for the nation and for the Pony. Russell's case, although it never came to trial, had seriously injured the company's good name with official Washington. Mr. Russell had made an announcement that the Pony would stop altogether on New Year's Day unless the company received the help it needed. But the Pony continued to run, in some mysterious way finding the means to make all its regular trips, slowed occasionally only by bad weather.

Creditors, seeing possible bankruptcy ahead for Russell, Majors, and Waddell, began to close in on the firm, hoping to collect at least a part of the huge amounts owed them before it was too late. In the *Deseret News* of Salt Lake City on February 27, 1861, there appeared a news story expressing alarm over the loss of the Pony:

> A few days since, there was a little excitement raised in this city, by the circulation of a report, that all the stock belonging to the Mail and Express Company in this Territory, had been attached at the suit of Livingston, Bell & Co.; in consequence of which, the Mail and Express would be stopped, and no further communications might be expected from the East very soon, which, in these exciting times would certainly be a great inconvenience, not to say calamity.

> The report that the animals had been attached, was correct, but we are credibly informed that there was no intention on the part of the Plaintiffs in the case, to interfere with the transmission of the mail, nor to prevent the "pony" from making its regular trips, for the present, at least, and not at all, if the matter of indebtedness shall be otherwise satisfactorily adjusted. If we rightly understand the matter, the transaction may be considered more favorable than otherwise, to the continuance of the existing mail and express arrangements.

Perhaps the backers of the Pony hoped for better treatment from the new administration than from the old for they were still carrying on when President-elect Lincoln took office on March 4, 1861. On that memorable day the Pony was called upon to begin the speedy delivery of Lincoln's inaugural message to the West.

March of 1861 was a month of heavy snows and mountain blizzards. The winter winds were still howling through the passes and sweeping

Storm Clouds in the East

[115]

The Pony Express

across the high plains of Nebraska and Wyoming when the Pony began the journey to the West. The future of California—the direction the state would take in the critical days just ahead—depended on the power of Lincoln's words and his unyielding stand on slavery.

Every man along the line realized the gravity of the moment. From the division superintendents, whose word was law, down through the ranks to the lowly stock-tenders, every one working for the Pony was prepared to see that Lincoln's message got through as fast as possible. Every station held ready the fastest horses, saved for the occasion, and every rider was aware that he was playing a role in a historical event.

The telegraph had been built by then as far west as Fort Kearny,

PRESIDENTIAL PARADE
While the presidential parade was still passing the Capitol grounds, the inaugural address was on its way by wire from Washington to the Pony Express terminus at Fort Kearney.

[116]

but 1600 miles lay from that point to the next telegraph station at Fort Churchill, Nevada. The rider who left Fort Kearny with the message had good weather. But as the Pony came closer and closer to the mountains, it ran straight into the kind of delaying weather that had been dreaded. Fortunately, extra men had been sent out to the stations to help keep the trail passable.

The trip was one of the hardest the Pony had ever made. It took seven days of hard going to get through to Salt Lake City, and another five to Fort Churchill, Nevada, where the news was put on the wire for San Francisco and Sacramento. Everyone was overjoyed to receive it, but little mention was made of the brave men who had battled storm, blizzard and snowdrift for twelve long days in order to bring it to them. By this time Californians were accustomed to the exploits of the Pony riders and so were not surprised by the performance.

The Pony Express had done a magnificent job from the beginning, overriding every obstacle with a spirit never equaled. Since it could not be downed by the elements or ruined by financial losses, perhaps, as the historian H. H. Bancroft believed, the Pony was the victim of trickery on the part of Southern partisans and business rivals. He was convinced that Russell, beset by money worries, had been trapped into an embarrassing position by friends of the Butterfield line. The success of the conspiracy had removed Butterfield's powerful rival once and for all. In *Chronicles of the Builders,* Bancroft had this to say about the scandal of the stolen bonds:

> While Russell was in Washington, endeavoring to secure some relief, he was induced to take $870,000 in bonds of the Interior Department, as a loan, and giving as security acceptances on the War Department, furnished him by Secretary Floyd, a part of which was not yet due. The bonds, as it turned out, were stolen by Godard Bailey, a family connection of Floyd's, and law clerk in the Interior Department. . . . In the temporary confusion which followed the discovery of the fraud, Russell lost his opportunity, as perhaps it was meant that he should.

Whatever the causes of Russell's failure to obtain a suitable contract, the Pony Express was to receive a severe blow when the Butterfield stage line was moved to the Central Route in the spring of 1861. The

Storm Clouds in the East

[1 1 7]

CARRYING LINCOLN'S INAUGURAL

ADDRESS ACROSS THE ROCKIES

The Pony Express

nearness of the Civil War had been sharply demonstrated to the owners of the Butterfield line by Confederate raids on the route. Livestock disappeared by the drove; stages were burned or confiscated. No longer did the red and green coaches, loaded to the axles with mailbags and jammed-in passengers, careen across Texas. By early March of 1861, travel on the Ox-Bow Route was at an end.

Congress acted with dispatch. The Central Route, already proven superior by the daring of the Pony Express, now became the desirable one. An emergency act recommended the transfer of the Butterfield line to that route and provided an annual pay of $1,000,000. The owners of the Pony Express were to share the profits.

An involved deal was worked out between Russell, Majors and Waddell and the Butterfield interests, now more generally known as the Overland Mail Company. It provided that the owners of the Pony would carry both mail and passengers from the Missouri River to Salt Lake City. The Overland Mail Company was given the same job for the rest of the way to California. A contract signed by Russell and William B. Dinsmore, president of the Overland Mail, stipulated that Russell, Majors and Waddell were to receive $470,000 for their part in the plan. The receipts from the Pony itself were to be divided equally between the firms.

For a little while longer the Pony would be the swiftest and most reliable link between East and West. At the same time several days had been cut from the schedule of the transcontinental stage coaches.

The financial affairs of the C.O.C. and P.P. Express Company, increasingly shaky as the expense of the Pony Express mounted, were only superficially improved by the new contract. Behind the scenes, Ben Holliday, the western promoter, advanced large sums of money to the company and was given a mortgage for security.

It was March of 1862, however, when the Pony backers, unable to meet the matured mortgage, saw their company sold at public auction in Leavenworth, Kansas. Ben Holliday bid the company in to protect his own interest.

Holliday was the most colorful of all the gaudy personalities produced by the frontier. He was jovial, aggressive and extravagant, and most of all a very able businessman. From the beginning of his career as a grog-shop and grocery-store keeper, everything he turned his hand to was successful.

Born in Kentucky, he came out to Missouri to seek his fortune. He did not have long to wait before starting his climb to the point where he was acclaimed, as Russell had been before him, the "Napoleon" of the plains.

Holliday was already well along in his career when he took over the C.O.C. and P.P. Express Company. He knew a lot about staging as well as ships and mining and he put the line on its feet in a short time. With a portion of the $1,000,000 subsidy at his command, he could afford to do things with a lavish hand. He bought more horses, put on new Concord coaches and hired more employees for the stations.

He also took care of his own tastes, which were royal. His coach was custom-built, and furnished in unusual fashion for his cross-country trips. A Pullman-like interior contained a mattress and an oil lamp with a reflector for reading and writing en route. In the daytime he rode outside with the driver.

Holliday kept a close watch on the Overland route, although his several residences were in the East. Two or three times a year he would make a tour of inspection along the entire line, taking the superintendent along. Sometimes a second coach carried servants, including a valet and cook.

He delighted in breaking all speed records for coach travel, no matter how much it cost him in worn-out horses and broken-down coaches. His special coach once carried him on a record ride which won him columns of publicity in the newspapers. It was a show trip from Sacramento to St. Joseph, with all the stations alerted in advance and the best stage horses held ready for the fancy vehicle. All ordinary stage travel had to stand by while the six-horse coach tore past at an unbelievable speed.

The trip was made in twelve days instead of the usual nineteen or twenty. Some people said he had been trying to outdo the Pony, but if so, he failed. More than likely he was trying to see how near he could approach the record of the Pony which he admired so greatly.

Storm Clouds in the East

CHAPTER 9

BAD MEN AND HEROES

THE OUTLAWS were having a holiday around Julesburg. Everything seemed to be playing into their hands. With the roads loaded with emigrant trains, stage coaches and Pony Expressmen, the highwaymen were enjoying a wide range of victims to prey upon. At Julesburg the trail forked, one branch going on up the Platte to Denver and Pike's Peak, the other west toward Fort Laramie.

Julesburg was the center of the lawless, riotous life west of Fort Kearney. It was to Julesburg and its honky-tonks that a wild assortment

The Pony Express

of traders, hunters, Indian fighters and road-agents came regularly to squander their money on a round of pleasure. There was talk, too, that it was in Julesburg that the highwaymen were getting advance information about especially rich wagon trains and stage coaches going on west.

Julesburg had taken its name and much of its character from Jules Reni, a hard drinking, bullying French Canadian, master of the stage station and just lately appointed division agent for the Pony Express. Jules had staked out his claim long before any settlement had even been thought of. As first citizen of the town he was hired by the Overland company to run a very tough section of the line—a rough man for a rough job.

Before long things in Jules' division began to go wrong. Stage schedules fell behind, livestock mysteriously disappeared. Time after time, wagon trains were attacked soon after leaving Julesburg. Men who lived through raids said there were sometimes white men painted and dressed as Indians in the attacking parties. Prisoners released from Indian camps told of visits from white men who mingled freely with the Indians and divided the loot with them. Everything pointed to cooperation between the outlaws and the men in charge of the big station in Julesburg. The belief grew that Jules was the leader of the desperadoes and was giving them information about travelers on the road.

When hints of Jules' activities reached the company officials, he was promptly fired. In his place came Jack Slade, who turned out to be tougher than Jules, but far more devoted to the interests of the company.

Not much was known about Slade except that he had fought in the Mexican war and that he insisted as being addressed as Captain Slade. There was gossip that he had killed a man or two during a drinking bout, but he looked and talked like a gentleman—too much so, according to the ideas of some.

Whatever Slade's background, Jules was all set to make it hot for him. Already angered over being replaced by Slade, he was insulted once again when Slade hired as an assistant Jules' own former employee and bitter enemy. When Slade repossessed some company horses Jules had taken for his own use, Reni reached the limits of his fury.

One day when Slade was not looking, Jules, standing behind a convenient door, filled him full of gunshot. Slade drew his pistol and managed to pump a couple of bullets into Jules before he fell to the floor. But

Jules had the better of it, and he was so slightly wounded that he was able to leave town for a while in order to let the townspeople forget his murderous ambush.

Slade did not die, but from his sickbed he swore he would cut off Jules' ears and wear them on his watch chain. His long trip to St. Louis to have the lead removed from his body did not lessen his desire for revenge. His return trip increased it, since at every stop he heard the same tale—that Jules was still gunning for him and had boasted everywhere that he would kill Slade on sight.

Slade, with a posse of picked men, ran Jules down at Pacific Springs and brought him back to Julesburg, bound hand and foot. Jules was not to have the privilege of the quick, clean death from hanging often given frontier outlaws. Instead, he was made fast to a snubbing post in a corral and then Slade demonstrated his shooting skill, using Jules for target practice before finishing him off altogether.

The way in which Slade got rid of Jules, made him a symbol of frontier brutality for decades. And nothing in his behavior before that time or after did anything to soften the picture. Slade would shoot first and ask questions later, when there was even a suspicion of horse stealing or stage hold-up.

Four highwaymen who had hidden away in a lonely ranch house, found out that his reputation for being a dead shot was well deserved. On that occasion Slade approached the house alone, kicked in the door and started shooting. His first shots killed two of the men and wounded a third. The fourth man jumped out of a window but had not gone fifty yards before he was brought down by Slade, firing through a window. It was such incidents that put the fear of law into the lawless element around Julesburg.

Slade worked hard at ridding the section of horse thieves and desperadoes. He was constantly traveling from one station to another, checking on rumors, taking into custody any employee who had even so much as given shelter to a suspicious character. Many men who knew conditions around Julesburg and on west to South Pass thought Slade's ruthless methods were needed.

As conditions in his division improved, his own character became more violent. When he was on a spree Slade became a demon to be avoided by both friends and strangers. Once he was said to have wiped

RENEGADE WHITES JO

NDIANS IN RAID

out an entire family because the husband had made some critical remarks about his treatment of Jules.

Strangely enough it was a rather small offense that caused Slade and his employers to part company. When Slade and some of his cronies shot holes in the canned goods in the sutler's store at Fort Halleck, the Overland company was forced by the military commandant there to give him his notice. Slade took the news calmly and in a few days had gone on his way.

Slade followed the new gold discoveries to Virginia City, Montana, where outlaws were in such complete control, that they had elected one of their group as sheriff. The Vigilance committee which was organized to clean up the lawless element was the undoing of Slade. In 1864 he was publicly hanged after threatening to shoot a judge of the Miner's Court.

JIM MOORE'S FAMOUS RIDE

It was trouble at the Julesburg station that brought about Jim Moore's famous ride. It all occurred because a rider had been foolish enough to tangle with one of the rough characters in Julesburg and had lost his life in the fight that followed.

In June, Moore, carrying Government dispatches from Washington, left Midway station for his long run to Julesburg. The papers in his mochila were marked urgent, and he made the one hundred and forty miles in especially fast time. Galloping up to the low log cabin that served as the express station, Moore learned that the rider scheduled to start eastward had been murdered.

As there was no one to substitute for the slain man except Moore, he started again, speeding back over the road he had left just a few minutes before. At Midway station he found he had covered the two hundred and eighty miles in a little less than fifteen hours, an average of eighteen miles an hour. He had set one of the best speed records made by a Pony Expressman.

WILD BILL'S CAREER

Another stage and Pony Express station was a scene of a shooting spree which became famous in both history and fiction. Wild Bill Hickok began his career as a hero of the Wild West when he finished off the McCanles gang at Rock Creek in Nebraska.

[128]

The Pony Express

Wild Bill, as fiction had it, was a dashing rider for the Pony Express. He saw something was wrong as soon as he came in sight of Rock Creek station on that hot, dusty day in the summer of 1861. There was not a soul in sight and no horse stood saddled and ready for him. Something dire must have happened to the station agent and his wife.

As he reined in before the cabin he heard a woman's blood-curdling screams and the familiar sounds of physical combat. Instinctively he drew his revolver, not a minute too soon. A burly figure appeared in the doorway. Wild Bill fired away. Another man came close behind the first and instantly there were two dead men instead of one. He was now drawing the fire of four more brigands. But Wild Bill still had two bullets left, one apiece for two of the quartet. His knife that he was never without did in the fifth.

It was now that Wild Bill noticed the body of the dead station keeper on the floor and in the same moment snatched the rifle from the hands of the corpse and dispatched the sixth and last gunman.

Leaving the distraught widow in the hands of travelers who had happened along at exactly the right moment, Wild Bill then sprang on his horse and was off like lightning, carrying the mail on west, taking the slaying of six men as part of the day's work. The "McCanles Gang" that Hickok had speeded into the next world so casually grew larger as the story was told and retold, sometimes having as many as eight members, sometimes more.

That several men were killed that day at Rock Creek, and that Wild Bill Hickok was responsible for their sudden departure, there was no question. Hickok was brought to trial and acquitted, and no doubt the whole affair would have ended there and been forgotten, if he had been an ordinary frontier killer.

But Wild Bill had greater things in store for him. A handsome, manly figure, Wild Bill stood six-feet-one in his Indian moccasins. His size would seem to make him a poor choice for a Pony rider, but clad in the fringed deerskin garments of the day, he was a romantic personage well suited for his role of frontier hero. Later on, when he had become famous as an Indian scout and a straight shooting cow town marshal, minor incidents in his early life were built into great adventures of the West.

The truth about the fracas at Rock Creek was very different from the thrilling story about Wild Bill's daring that was told and embroidered

Bad Men and Heroes

[129]

The Pony Express

along the trail. David McCanles, who lost his life that hot day at Rock Creek, was a Nebraska farmer. Wild Bill Hickok was in 1861 simply James Butler Hickok, an unknown man of twenty-three, engaged in the most menial job to be done at Rock Creek station. Dock Brink, who took care of the livestock, had hired him as an assistant when the youth came out from Illinois to try his luck on the frontier. Hickok fed and watered the horses and mules and did odd jobs around the stable.

The station, a lean-to log cabin, had been built by McCanles, who later sold the building to the Pony company. When notes came due and were left unpaid, McCanles blamed the station agent, Horace Wellman, and accused him of putting the money into his own pocket. McCanles, an overbearing and argumentative man, had also made a bitter enemy of Hickok. He had given him the insulting nickname of Duck Bill, thus calling attention to Hickok's protruding upper lip.

One afternoon in July, McCanles, accompanied by two neighbors and his twelve-year-old son, went to the station to tell Wellman that he could no longer postpone making payment for the station. A brawl developed and before it was over McCanles and his friends were dead.

The boy got away safely after seeing his father shot down. In his later life the son insisted that the three men had been killed in cold blood, that they had gone completely unarmed and had been attacked by Hickok without reason.

Somewhere in between the two stories lay truth. Men who knew Hickok thought the second version was as impossible as the first, since Hickok was never known to do any unnecessary killing and was noted for his bravery and fairness. In any case he had unwittingly provided material for the fictioneers of the early West who endowed the Pony riders, real or imaginary, with superhuman qualities, almost from birth.

BUFFALO BILL'S FEATS

Billy Cody, the future Buffalo Bill, shared honors with Wild Bill as a legendary hero of the plains. Cody, who once briefly carried messages between the freighting trains of Russell, Majors and Waddell when he was fourteen, turned up as the leading character in Colonel Prentiss Ingraham's extravagant best-seller, *The Pony Express Rider; or Buffalo Bill's Frontier Feats*. For extra glamor Ingraham even had Cody and

[130]

Wild Bill making the western trek together, two shiny-faced youths, facing all hazards with fortitude and skill:

> One day when he had ridden into Leavenworth, Buffalo Billy met his old friend, Wild Bill, who was fitting out a train with supplies for the Overland Stage Company, and he was at once persuaded to join him in the trip West, going as assistant wagon master. . . . On his trip West with Wild Bill he had carried his books, and often in camp he had whiled away the time in studying, until he was asked if he was reading for a lawyer or a preacher.
>
> But when well away from civilization his books were cast aside for his rifle, and he was constantly in the saddle supplying the train with game.

Billy Cody was only fourteen when the Pony Express started, and the fact of his extreme youth was the only bit of realism in the following dialogue between Billy and the notorious Slade of Julesburg. The stage is set when Billy presents a fictional letter of recommendation from Mr. Russell and asks to be hired as a rider. Slade speaks first:

> "I would like to oblige you, my boy, but you are too young, the work kills strong men in a short time."
>
> "Give me a trial, sir, please, for I think I can pull through," said Billy.
>
> "But are you used to hard riding and a life of danger?"
>
> "Yes, sir, I've secn hard work, young as I am."
>
> "I see now that Russell says you are Buffalo Billy," and Slade glanced again at the letter.
>
> "Yes, sir, that's what my pards call me."
>
> "I have heard of you, and you can become a Pony rider; if you break down you can give it up."
>
> The very next day Billy was set to work on the trail from Red Buttes on the North Platte, to Three Crossings on the Sweet Water, a distance of seventy-six miles.
>
> It was a very long piece of road, but Billy did not weaken, and ere long became known as the Boss Pony Rider.

Ingraham goes on to develop the adventures that gave Billy the right to be called Boss Rider. They might have surprised the true Pony

The Pony Express

riders, and no doubt would have made them smile. These included a ride of three hundred and twenty-two miles without rest, encounters with highwaymen and Indians, near scalpings and miraculous hair-breadth escapes, all in rapid succession, or even simultaneously. Before long the work was too tame for Billy and he wanted a change. His

Every tale that came out of the West was turned into popular fiction and exaggerated beyond the point of credibility. Beadle's Pony Express rider turned out to be Buffalo Bill Cody, who never was a real Pony rider.

luck held, and even the way he changed jobs was sheer melodrama. Ingraham describes Billy's valor in risking all for the stage company that had employed him in order to prove himself worthy to hold the reins of an Overland stage coach:

One day as he sped along like the wind he saw ahead of him the stage coach going at full speed and no one on the box.

At once he knew there was trouble, and as he drew nearer he discovered some Indians dash out of a ravine and give chase.

As he heard the clatter of hoofs behind him he looked around and saw a dozen red-skins coming in pursuit . . .

The stage coach was now in the open prairie, and dashing along the trail as fast as the horses could go, while the Indians in close pursuit numbered but three.

Billy was well mounted upon a sorrel mare, and urging her with the spur he soon came in range of the red-skin furthest in the rear and hastily fired.

Down went the pony, and the Indian was thrown with such violence that he was evidently stunned, as he lay where he had fallen.

Another shot wounded one of the remaining Indians, and they hastily sped away to the right obliquie in flight, while Billy dashed on to the side of the coach.

There were five passengers within, and two of them were women, and all were terribly frightened, though evidently not knowing that their driver lay dead upon the box, the reins still grasped in his nerveless hands.

Riding near, Billy seized his mail bags and dextrously got from his saddle to the stage, and the next instant he held the reins in his firm grip.

He knew well that Ted Remus, the driver, had carried out a box of gold, and was determined to save it for the company if in his power.

His horse, relieved of his weight and trained to run the trail, kept right on ahead, and he, skillfully handling the reins, for he was a fine driver, drove on at the topmost speed of the six animals drawing the coach.

[133]

The Pony Express

Behind him came the Indians, steadily gaining; but Billy plied the silk in a style that made his team fairly fly, and they soon reached the hills.

Here the red-skins again gained, for the road was not good and in many places very dangerous.

But once over the ridge, and just as the Indians were near enough to fill the back of the coach with arrows, Billy made his team jump ahead once more, and at breakneck speed they rushed down the steep road, the vehicle swaying wildly, and the passengers within not knowing whether they would be dashed to pieces, or scalped by the Indians, or which death would be the most to be desired. But Billy, in spite of his lightning driving, managed his team well, and after a fierce run of half an hour rolled up to the door of the station in a style that made the agent and the lookers-on stare.

No matter how sensational the popular novels became, their mythical heroes hardly endured greater perils than the real Pony riders. Over stifling deserts where the air was white with alkali dust, through swollen rivers and desolate mountain passes the expressmen made their way, never stopping to consider the hazards that lay ahead of them.

FAMOUS TRUE ADVENTURES

Ingraham found many true incidents to use in his romantic version of a Pony rider's life. One from Utah may have furnished him with an idea or two. Richard Erastus Egan, whose run lay between Salt Lake and Rush Valley, one day came upon what at first appeared to be an abandoned stage coach. On closer inspection he found the driver dead on the box, and inside the lifeless passengers lay sprawled on the seats. It was plain that the same brigands who had shot the travelers had made off with the stage horses. Indians loitered in the vicinity, and one of them now turned and galloped toward Egan.

Egan, aware that he had the superior mount, fled, always keeping the Indian at a safe distance. When he felt he had tired the Indian's mustang sufficiently, he turned abruptly and sped toward the pursuing brave, who was completely thrown off guard by Egan's trick. As Egan advanced directly upon him, shouting and brandishing his revolver, the hostile Indian sped away as fast as he could go.

[134]

Nick Wilson, another of the Mormon boys who rode through an unsettled stretch of Utah, had several close calls before an Indian's aim proved good enough to affect him. A Goshute Indian one day took careful aim and imbedded an arrow in Wilson's forehead, but without serious consequences. Alex Carlyle was luckier when an Indian's bullet merely knocked his cap off.

By the spring of 1861 another tribe of Indians was causing the Pony riders some anxiety. The Sioux, whose hunting grounds in Wyoming had been invaded again and again by white men, were on the war path. One day when Henry Avis was on the point of leaving the station at Mud Springs for his run to Horseshoe Creek, he was told that bands of Indian braves had been seen along the trail. He arrived at Horseshoe Creek surprised that he had encountered none.

A stage coach had pulled into the station just before Avis, and the driver told of seeing a raiding party near Deer Creek. Avis' relief had not shown up and it was up to him to continue on straight into the path of the Sioux war party. Taking a fresh horse, Avis went on his way, cutting across country, in an effort to fool any warriors waiting in ambush. In this manner he reached Deer Creek station to find that the expected Indian raid was over.

The station men had been fortunate. This particular Indian party had limited its foray to stealing horses and mules, and had left the frightened station attendants unharmed. No doubt the nearness of Fort Laramie had been a great factor in discouraging a bloody raid on the lonely station. While a certain amount of horse stealing was accepted and overlooked, the Sioux knew that murders and scalpings would bring a company of cavalrymen in deadly pursuit.

There was never anything dull about riding for the Pony. The dashing riders generated their own interest and hardly needed "fixing up" in any extravagant fiction.

Mark Twain, who journeyed out to Nevada by stage, described the excitement of seeing a Pony Expressman appear on the horizon, come closer and closer and finally streak by in one breathtaking instant. *Roughing It* contains this account of the Pony rider and his horse:

> In a little while all interest was taken up in stretching our
> necks and watching for the "pony-rider"—the fleet messenger
> who sped across the continent from St. Joe to Sacramento,

Bad Men and Heroes

[135]

The Pony Express

carrying letters nineteen hundred miles in eight days! Think of that for perishable horse and human flesh and blood to do!

The pony-rider was usually a little bit of a man, brimful of spirit and endurance. No matter what time of the day or night his watch came on, and no matter whether it was winter or summer, raining, snowing, hailing, or sleeting, or whether his "beat" was a level straight road or a crazy trail over mountain crags and precipices, or whether it led through peaceful regions or regions that swarmed with hostile Indians, he must be always ready to leap into the saddle and be off like the wind!

There was no idling-time for a pony-rider on duty. He rode fifty miles without stopping, by daylight, moonlight, starlight, or through the blackness of darkness—just as it happened.

He rode a splendid horse that was born for a racer and fed and lodged like a gentleman; kept him at his utmost speed for ten miles, and then, as he came crashing up to the station where stood two men holding fast a fresh, impatient steed, the transfer of rider and mailbag was made in a twinkling of an eye, and away flew the eager pair and were out of sight before the spectator could get hardly the ghost of a look.

The stage-coach traveled about a hundred to a hundred and twenty-five miles a day (twenty-four hours), and pony-rider about two-hundred and fifty. There were about eighty pony-riders in the saddle all the time, night and day, stretching in a long, scattering procession from Missouri to California, forty flying eastward, and forty toward the west, and among them making four hundred gallant horses earn a stirring livelihood and see a deal of scenery every single day in the year.

We had had a consuming desire, from the beginning, to see a pony-rider, but somehow or other all that passed us and all that met us managed to streak by us in the night, and so we heard only a whiz and a hail, and the swift phantom of the desert was gone before we could get our heads out of the windows. But now we were expecting one along every moment, and would see him in broad daylight. Presently the driver exclaims: *"Here he comes!"*

[136]

Every neck is stretched further, and every eye strained wider. Away across the endless dead level of the pairie a black speck appears against the sky, and it is plain that it moves. Well, I should think so! In a second or two it becomes a horse and rider, rising nearer—growing more and more distinct, more and more sharply defined—nearer and still nearer, and the flutter of the hoofs comes faintly to the ear—another instant a whoop and a hurrah from our upper deck, a wave of the rider's hand, but no reply, and man and horse burst past our excited faces, and go winging away like a belated fragment of a storm!

So sudden is it all, and so like a flash of unreal fancy, that but for the flake of white foam left quivering and perishing on a mail-sack after the vision had flashed by and disappeared, we might have doubted whether we had seen any actual horse and man at all, maybe.

Bad Men and Heroes

CHAPTER 10

THE END OF THE TRAIL

It took the telegraph to stop the Pony Express finally. In the summer of 1861, when work crews began to plant poles along the line of the transcontinental telegraph, the Pony entered the last stage of its fabulous career.

A lot of effort and planning had preceded the actual building of the telegraph line to the West. Even before the gold-rush began, someone a long way ahead of his time, had said it should be built and had been called an impractical fool.

The Pony Express

In 1852, Henry O'Rielly, a power in the telegraph world, went much further. In a petition presented before the Senate, O'Rielly outlined his plans for stringing a telegraph wire from the Missouri river to California, at his own risk and expense. He asked only for one kind of support from the Federal government—protection from Indian attack. Even this was refused and O'Rielly dropped the project. He had set the ball rolling, however, and from that time onward, businessmen and statesmen, the latter usually from the state of California, never let the idea die.

A couple of years later, Hiram Sibley, the president of the new but important Western Union Company, tried to persuade his own firm to undertake the venture and got a flat refusal from his board of directors. They were more than willing to see some other firm take a chance on going bankrupt but they had no intention of risking their own capital and prestige on anything so uncertain.

All the old arguments against the construction of the telegraph were given a new airing, with emphasis on the impossibility of getting the necessary supplies into the interior of the country. Wire and insulators would have to be hauled long distances overland or taken by sea around Cape Horn to San Francisco. From that city they would be carried up over the Sierras to the construction crews. For some sections of the line, poles would have to be carried by wagon over long, rutted roads. Most of Sibley's associates thought that even if the poles were erected they would have little chance of staying in place. The Indians would delight in chopping them down or merely burning them on the spot. Endless repairs would be necessary in the remotest regions of the West. And if the lines could be kept open, it was thought very few people would use the service at the high prices that would be necessary.

Sibley had to wait a while longer, but in 1860 he placed his scheme for a western wire line before Congress and got excellent results. The time was ripe for an overland telegraph and in June of that year, Congress approved the bill which would "facilitate communication between the Atlantic and the Pacific States by electric telegraph." Sibley was given the contract, which carried a subsidy of $40,000 a year for ten years. It also specified that the transcontinental line be built within two years from July, 1860, and that government agencies would receive priority in its use.

Two new companies were formed for the actual building of the telegraph. In the East, Sibley and Jephtha Wade headed the Pacific Telegraph Company which would construct the line east of Salt Lake City. In California, the four pioneer telegraph companies of the state consolidated to form the Overland Telegraph Company. West of Salt Lake City, the Overland Company would have full responsibility for establishing the transcontinental line.

Much thought had been given to the route that the line would take. Edward Creighton, a telegraph contractor who had built many lines in the East, spent the fall and winter of 1860 surveying and observing the road the telegraph wire would follow. Sibley had already taken a chance on the telegraph's future and had extended the line as far west as Fort Kearney in the fall of 1860. It was at that point that Creighton began the careful gathering of information about the terrain in general, timber stands to provide telegraph poles, and water supplies for the work crews that would be laboring through the heat of summer. Creighton made the long trip alone, traveling much of the way on horseback. As he made his way up the Platte valley and on through South Pass to Salt Lake he followed the route of the Pony Express.

The End of the Trail

BEGINNING OF THE END
Day by day as the telegraph wire was stretched farther, the Pony Express became less and less important.

The Pony Express

The building of the western section of the line was off to a good start by early summer of 1861. It had taken James Gamble, the superintendent in charge, a full month to bring his supply wagons and work crews across the Sierras to Carson City, the wire end. Constantly delayed by traffic on the mountain roads, the heavy wagons loaded with supplies for the weeks ahead, had finally reached Carson City late in June. Half of the work force was then sent ahead to Salt Lake City and from that time on the two work gangs advanced toward each other at a steady rate.

The same system was used on the eastern portion of the construction. Edward Creighton, general superintendent for the territory east of Salt Lake City, was overseer for a seven hundred mile stretch west of Fort Kearney, and W. H. Stebbins bossed the remaining four hundred miles.

On July Fourth, Creighton watched the setting of the first pole on his section of the line. From then on the work progressed rapidly, each crew averaging anywhere from three to eight miles a day. First the holes were dug, then close behind the laborers who had prepared the way came the pole setters. A crew of four or five men raised the pole into position and secured it firmly in the earth. Sometimes, because of the dry, loose quality of the soil, the pole had to be held fast by piles of rocks placed at its base. Last came the wire party with ladders and great reels of wire mounted on their wagons, ready for the final stage of stringing the wire. One day, when working through desert country, sixteen miles of poles, of twenty-five poles per mile were erected in order to reach a spot where water could be had before evening.

The western Indians were on their best behavior while the work crews were in the field. Later on they enjoyed a period of burning poles and ripping wires from their moorings, but during the actual building they caused very little trouble. The large numbers of Pony Express stations along the way, with their rough, well-armed keepers on hand at all hours, no doubt were a restraining influence on the young braves.

But Creighton did not rely on chance and the Pony Express stations for protection. He wanted to frighten the Indians away from the poles and the workmen once and for all. In order to impress the Indians with the magical power of the talking wire, he used the simplest and most logical means at his command. He let two Indian chiefs communicate by wire.

At Fort Kearney and Fort Laramie the tribal heads sent questions and answers back and forth and then sped away to a central meeting place to compare notes and see if they had been tricked. When they learned that they had really sent messages by the wire, no doubt remained in their minds that a spirit traveled along the wire. It was magic enough to fill them with fear of offending the spirit. It was Big Medicine, indeed. The word spread among the tribes like wildfire.

WHITE MAN'S MAGIC
The Indian imagined that he could hear voices in the telegraph pole.

Blankets, clothing and food were sometimes given to the Indians to keep them friendly, and occasionally Indians were hired to take care of the oxen and mules that pulled the wagons. One of these employees had an experience which added to the telegraph's mysterious reputation.

He was standing by one day when the wire stringing process was going on at a fast rate through Nevada. A thunder storm came up suddenly but the workmen continued in spite of the lightning flashing all around them. Well protected by the heavy buckskin gloves they were wearing, they had nothing to fear. The Indian, seeing that a little extra

[143]

The Pony Express

help was needed, decided to assist in tightening the wire and grabbed it with his bare hands.

The shock he received was multiplied by the fact that he stood barefoot on wet ground. He took off down the road as though a pack of wolves were at his heels. The men who saw him make his getaway, knew that they would never have any Indian difficulties in that particular section.

Each day the telegraph station at the head of the line advanced a few miles farther. Like a desert nomad the operator found himself in a new spot daily, set up in a tent or the corner of a way station.

By the early part of August, the Pony rider picked up east bound telegrams at Dry Creek station in eastern Nevada. A month later the eastern section of the line was reported finished as far west as Julesburg.

DEEP FORD
The magazines contemporary with the Pony Express pictured the rider in a very romantic way. Although he usually dressed in everyday clothes suited to the weather, some artists depicted him in fancy dress.

News dispatches taken off the wire at those points were transferred to the waiting mochila, just as they formerly had been at the starting point of Saint Joseph.

By October it looked as if it would be only a matter of days before the two lines being constructed from East and West would be joined. Then James Gamble, in charge of the western end, ran into trouble. With only fifty or sixty miles of the line in Utah still unfinished Gamble ran out of poles and found it impossible to buy any. Seasoned mountaineers, knowing that blizzards might descend upon them in October, had refused to go into the mountains to cut down trees. Gamble was aware that if he failed in this small stretch of the construction, he would be blamed for holding up the finish until the following spring.

Gamble sent out twenty wagons with a company of his own men to search for poles near Egan Canyon. A few days went by without any word from them. Then a note came by coach, saying that they had stopped at Egan Canyon and had refused to go up into the mountains to look for poles due to the lateness of the season.

Gamble set out in a stage coach for Egan Canyon, determined to hold the men to their original agreement to finish the job, no matter what the circumstances. He found them hard to convince and finally was forced to accompany them on the urgent mission.

Two or three days were required to find enough poles to finish the construction job but once the wagons were filled and the crew started on its way back down the mountain the finish of the big project was in sight.

On October 17, 1861, the line between Fort Kearney and Salt Lake City was completed and less than a week later it was possible to send a telegram from San Francisco to New York. The first message wired to New York from the West was a poetic one: "The Pacific to the Atlantic sends greetings; and may both oceans be dry before a foot of all the land that lies between them, shall belong to any other than one united country."

On October 26, the Pony Express came to its official end, although it actually continued to run for almost another month. It had amazed the nation with its spectacular performance but it could not compete with the lightning speed of the transcontinental telegraph. As the line of the telegraph poles lengthened across the country, the Pony carried

The Pony Express

fewer and fewer of the press dispatches about the Civil War, less and less of the urgent mail dealing with big business transactions. Along the trail which led from the Missouri to the Pacific, the clicking of telegraph keys supplanted the pounding hoof-beats of the Pony.

The Pony Express ran for only a year and a half, but in that short time it stirred the imaginations of men and women the world over. Every news story carrying the line "By Pony Express", every letter which had a Pony Express stamp attached, had a special meaning for the reader as he pictured the dashing rider speeding across the plains. Whether in New York, San Francisco, London or Paris, the reader felt it was his personal courier who was braving the dangers of the wild and desolate West. The Pony's brave horsemen lifted the Pony Express above the level of a business undertaking and into the realm of romantic adventure.

COTTONWOOD STATION
This station on the Hollenberg ranch
was also known as Hollenberg Station

RIDERS FOR THE PONY EXPRESS

Henry Avis
Melville Baughn
James Beatley
Charles Becker
"Boston"
William Boulton
John Brandenberger
Hugh Brown
James Bucklin
John Burnett
William Campbell
Alex Carlisle
William Carr
William Carrigan
Bill Cates
Jimmy Clark
"Deadwood Dick" Clarke
Richard Cleve
Charles Cliff
Gus Cliff
"Sawed-off Jim" Cumbo
Louis Dean
Joe Donovan
W. E. Dorrington
Calvin Downs
James E. Dunlap
Howard Egan
Erastus Egan
J. K. Ellis
H. J. Faust
John Fisher

William Fisher
Johnnie Frey
George Gardner
Jim Gentry
Jim Gilson
Sam Gilson
Frank Gould
Billy Hamilton
Robert Haslam
Martin Hogan
Let. Huntington
"Irish Tom"
William James
David R. Jay
Will D. Jenkins
Sam S. Jobe
Jack Keetley
Jay G. Kelley
Mike Kelly
Thomas Owen King
John Koerner
"Little Yank"
Bob Martin
J. G. McCall
James McDonald
Jim McNaughton
Bill McNaughton
Jim Moore
J. H. Murphy
Josh Perkins
William Pridham

Thomas Ranahan
Theodore Rand
James Randall
Thomas Reynolds
Johnson "Billy" Richardson
Bart Riles
Don C. Rising
Harry Roff
Edward Rush
G. G. Sangiovanni
John Seerbeck
John Sinclair
George Spurr
W. H. Streeper
Robert C. Strickland
William Strohm
John W. Suggett
George Thacher
Charles P. Thompson
James M. Thompson
George Towne
Warren Upson
William E. van Blaricon
Henry Wallace
Dan Westcott
Michael M. Whelan
H. C. Willis
Nick Wilson
Henry Worley
Jose Zowgaltz

[147]

VALLEY OF THE GREAT SALT LAKE

THROUGH THE SOUTH PASS

Humboldt

Sulp
Robert's Cr
Cold Sra
Dry Creek
Cape Horn
Simpson's Park
Reese River
Mt Airy
Castle Rock
Edward's Ck
Cold Spr
Middle Ck
Fairview
Mountain Well
Stillwater
Old River
Bucks
Nevada
Desert Well
Drytown

SALAMENTO PASSING OLD FORT SUTTER

Lake Tahoe

Strawberry
Webster's
Yank's
Moss
Sportsmanshall
Placerville
Folsom
Mills

Carson
Genoa
Fridays

SACRAMENTO

SAN FRANCISCO

THROUGH SNOW OVER THE SIERRAS

CALIFORNIA   NEVADA

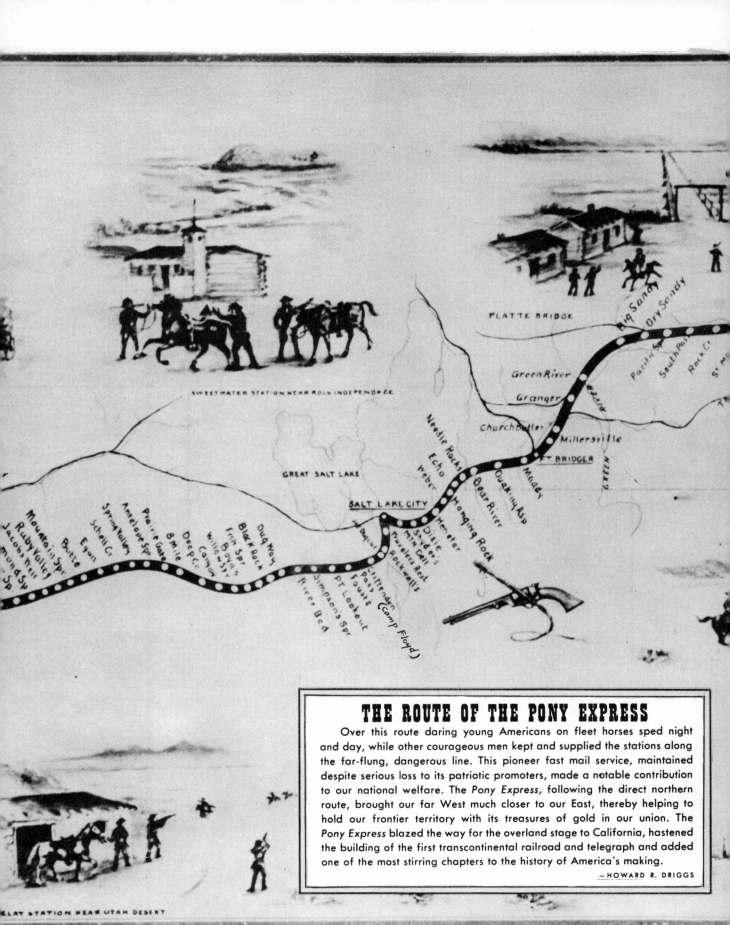

SWEETWATER STATION NEAR ROCK INDEPENDECE.

PLATTE BRIDGE

Big Sandy
Dry Sandy
Pacific Spr.
South Pass
Rock Cr.
St. M

Green River
Granger
Church Buttes
Millersville
FT. BRIDGER
Muddy
Quaking Asp
GREEN RIVER

Needle Rocks
Echo
Weber
Hanging Rock
Bear River

GREAT SALT LAKE

SALT LAKE CITY

Dixie
Snyder's
Mtn. Dell
Travelers Rest
Rockwell's

Dug Way
Black Rock
Fish Spr.
Boyd's
Willow Spr.
Canyon
Deep Cr.
8 Mile
Prairie Gate
Schell Cr.
Antelope Spr.
Spring Valley
Egan
Butte
Ruby Valley
Mountain Spr.
Jacob's Well
mon & Sp.

Deep Cr.
Crittenden
Pass
Fausts
Pt. Lookout
Fausts (Camp Floyd)
Simpson's Spr.
River Bed

KLAY STATION NEAR UTAH DESERT

UTAH

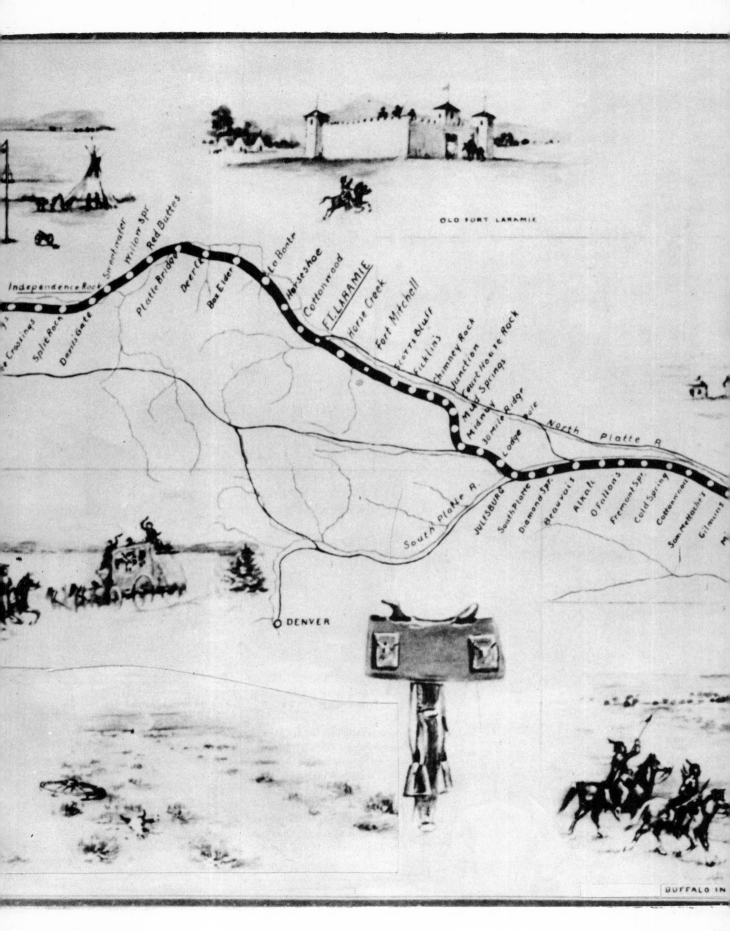

OLD FORT LARAMIE

Independence Rock   Sweetwater   Willow Spr.   Red Buttes   Platte Bridge   Deer Ck   Box Elder   La Bonte   Horseshoe   Cottonwood   FT. LARAMIE   Horse Creek   Fort Mitchell   Scotts Bluff   Ficklin's   Chimney Rock   Junction   Court House Rock   Mud Springs   Midway   30 mile Ridge   Lodge Pole   North Platte R.   JULESBURG   South Platte   Diamond Spr.   Beauvais   Alkali   O'fallons   Fremont Spr.   Cold Spring   Cottonwood   San McNachers   Gilmans

Split Rock   Devils Gate   South Platte R.   ○ DENVER

BUFFALO IN

WYOMING   COLORADO

CHIMNEY ROCK

COURT HOUSE ROCK

COLUMBUS

OMAHA COUNCIL BLUFFS

OLD FORT KEARNY

NEBRASKA CITY

Gilmans
Midway
Pillar Spr.
Plum Cr.
Craigs
Platte Sta.
FT. KEARNY
Hooks
Summit
Lone Tree
32 m Creek
Liberty farm
Kiowa
Thompsons
Big Sandy
Rock Creek
Hollenberg
MARYSVILLE
Guittards
Seneca
Log Chain
Granada
Kickapoo
Kennekuk
Troy
Elwood

ST. JOSEPH

ATCHISON
LEAVENWORTH

TOPEKA

KANSAS CITY

VEY OF THE PLATTE

Map Courtesy of Howard R. Driggs, President of the American Pioneer Trails Association

NEBRASKA   KANSAS   MISSOURI

One of the first Pony Express Stamps

ACKNOWLEDGMENT

The author wishes to acknowledge gratefully the assistance of the following historical societies, museums and libraries in tracking down old engravings, drawings, prints and paintings showing the Pony Express as it really was:

Kansas State Historical Society, Wells Fargo Bank History Room, Wyoming State Archives and Historical Department, Public Library of Denver, Nebraska State Historical Society, Library of Congress, Rare Book and American History Rooms of the New York Public Library.

Many individuals have also contributed invaluable and generous help in the research. The author wishes especially to thank the following: Miss Dorothy Gardiner, Mr. Allen Ottley of the California State Library at Sacramento, Mr. A. R. Mortensen of the Utah State Historical Society, the Hon. Mr. Charles Mabey, former governor of Utah, and Mr. Sylvester L. Vigilante, formerly head of the American History Room of the New York Public Library, now associated with the New York Historical Society.

PICTURE CREDITS

Frontispiece. London Illustrated News

Page

5. Hutchings California Magazine, July, 1860. California State Library
7. From a painting by Frederic Remington. Remington Art Memorial
8. California Mercantile Journal, 1860. California State Library
9. American History Room. New York Public Library
10-11. From a painting by H. W. Hansen. California Historical Society
14. A Tour of Duty in California. Joseph W. Revere. 1849
15. Thirty Years of Army Life on the Border. Randolph B. Marcy
16. California Mercantile Journal, 1860. California State Library
17. Frost's Pictorial History of California. Library of Congress
19. From a Currier and Ives lithograph. California Historical Society
21. Wells Fargo Bank History Room, San Francisco
24-25. Library of Congress
26. American History Room. New York Public Library
30. Stokes Collection. New York Public Library
31. California Mercantile Journal, 1860. California State Library
32. Print Room. New York Public Library
33. Library of Congress
34. American History Room. New York Public Library (top)
34. American History Room. New York Public Library
35. Library of Congress
36. Chips Off the Old Block. Alonzo Delano
37. Penknife Sketches. Alonzo Delano
38. New York Historical Society
40. Uncle Sam's Camels. Edited by Lewis B. Lesley
41. Uncle Sam's Camels. Edited by Lewis B. Lesley

[153]

BOOKS ON THE PERIOD OF THE PONY EXPRESS

Bancroft, Hubert H. *Chronicles of the Builders of the Commonwealth*. San Francisco; 1891-2.

Banning, William and George H. *Six Horses*. The Century Co., N.Y.; 1930.

Bradley, Glenn D. *The Story of the Pony Express*. A. C. McClurg and Co.; 1913.

Chapman, Arthur. *The Pony Express*. G. P. Putnam's Sons; 1932.

Driggs, Howard R. and Wilson, E. N. *The White Indian Boy*. World Book Company; 1919.

Egan, Howard. *Pioneering the West*. Howard R. Egan Estate, Richmond, Utah; 1917.

Gardiner, Dorothy. *West of the River*. Thomas Y. Crowell; 1941.

Hafen, Leroy R. *The Overland Mail*. Arthur H. Clark Co., Cleveland; 1926.

Harlow, Alvin F. *Old Waybills*. D. Appleton-Century Company; 1934.

Larimer, William and William H. H. *Reminiscences*. Privately printed, Pittsburgh; 1918.

Lesley, Lewis B., Editor. *Uncle Sam's Camels*. Harvard University Press.

Lewis, Oscar. *Sea Routes to the Gold Fields*. Alfred A. Knopf; 1949.

Majors, Alexander. *Seventy Years on the Frontier*. Rand, McNally and Company; 1893.

Paden, Irene D. *Wake of the Prairie Schooner*. The MacMillan Company; 1943.

Page, Elizabeth. *Wagons West: A Story of the Oregon Trail*. New York; 1930.

Paxon, F. L. *Last American Frontier*. New York; 1910.

Richardson, A. D. *Beyond the Mississippi*. Hartford, Conn.; 1867.

Root, Frank A. and Connelley, William E. *The Overland Stage to California*. Topeka; 1901.

Rusling, J. F. *Across America*. New York; 1875;

Sage, Rufus B. *Rocky Mountain Life*. Dayton, Ohio; 1857.

Simpson, J. H. *Report of Explorations Across Great Basin of Territory of Utah*. Washington; 1876.

Stimson, A. L. *History of Express Companies*. New York; 1858.

Thompson, Rob't L. *Wiring a Continent*. 1947.

Tullidge, E. W. *History of Salt Lake City*. Salt Lake City; 1886.

Twain, Mark. *Roughing It*. Harper and Brothers, New York.

Visscher, William Lightfoot. *A Thrilling and Truthful History of the Pony Express*. Rand, McNally and Co.; 1908.

Wiltsee, Ernest A. *Gold Rush Steamers*. The Grabhorn Press; 1938.

Wissler, Clark. *Indians of the United States*. Doubleday; 1940.